COLLECTIBLES

BOOKS BY MARIAN KLAMKIN

American Glass Bottles
Made in Occupied Japan: A Collector's Guide
The Carnival Glass Collector's Price Guide
The Collector's Guide to Carnival Glass
Watertown, Then and Now
The Return of Lafayette (1824–1825)
Old Sheet Music
Marine Antiques
The Depression Glass Collector's Price Guide
The Collector's Guide to Depression Glass

Picture Postcards
American Patriotic and Political China
Hands To Work: Shaker Folk Art and Industries
White House China
The Collector's Book of Bottles
The Collector's Book of Art Nouveau
The Collector's Book of Wedgwood
The Collector's Book of Boxes
Flower Arrangements That Last
Flower Arranging for Period Decoration

(with Charles Klamkin)

Investing in Antiques and Popular Collectibles for Pleasure and Profit
Wood Carvings: North American Folk Sculpture

COLLECTIBLES
A Compendium

MARIAN KLAMKIN

Photographs by Charles Klamkin

DOLPHIN BOOKS
Doubleday & Company, Inc.
Garden City, New York
1981

Library of Congress Cataloging in Publication Data

Klamkin, Marian.
  Collectibles: a compendium.

  Includes index.
  1. Collectors and collecting.   I. Title.
AM231.K52   069.5
ISBN: 0-385-12176-8
Library of Congress Catalog Card Number 77–27677

CONTENTS

INTRODUCTION

People are collecting today as never before. Stories about empty beer cans and other seemingly valueless objects selling for prices in four figures have made it hard to throw anything out and publicity about treasures found in attics and basements has encouraged noncollectors to rummage through every old box and trunk. Long lines form wherever auction houses set up appraisal desks. Financial writers bombard us with articles about the growing number of people who are turning to investment in "tangibles" as an alternative to more conventional ways of saving money.

There are many who would like to be involved in the world of collecting, but don't know how to begin. Others have fallen prey to advertisements and promotions for new collectibles in which they invest money regularly only to find out that what they have bought is worthless and has little or no value in the secondary market. These are people who have not been willing to do the necessary research and reading before they invest in collectibles. The collector who is not willing to study before spending money can be just as hurt as someone who plunges into the stock market without obtaining professional advice.

It is not always easy to find out what to collect or where to go to obtain the source material necessary to learn everything you need to know about special collecting fields. Those who have unlimited funds can easily purchase expert advice in order to invest in established collecting specialties where they can be assured that their purchases will increase in value with time. Those with limited funds search for collecting areas in which they might already have some interest and expertise. The burden of learning what they need to know about their investment is their responsibility and it is incumbent for them to read all available information before they invest.

It is not always easy to find the source material you need for specialized collecting areas. Many of the books and journals written about antiques and popular collectibles are published privately and sold only through the mail or by a few specialized book dealers. Good books published by major publishers often go out of print because marketing people do not understand the special ways in which books on antiques and collectibles are sold. Many are sold through distributors who specialize only in books on antiques and collectibles. Others are sold by itinerant book dealers who set up at antique shows or specialized collectors' shows sponsored by clubs and collecting organizations.

Because of the present rate of inflation, early retirements, and more leisure time, the field of antiques and popular collectibles includes thousands of new enthusiasts. New collecting specialties have become popular and prices have gone steadily upward for some of the more established collector's items. The increase in attendance at antique shows, flea markets, and auctions is evidence of the tremendous depth of interest in all areas of collecting. Because of this enthusiasm, people with a common interest in coins, stamps, bottles, advertising items, Depression era glassware, picture postcards, old cameras and images, or political memorabilia have formed clubs. Some of these clubs are regional or local, while others are international. The groups publish newsletters, hold shows and sales, and often conduct auctions among their members by mail or telephone.

The collectors' clubs and organizations

dedicated to one specialty provide an opportunity to trade surplus material, to exchange information, and to socialize with people who have similar interests. Some regional clubs meet on a monthly basis, while others meet annually or semiannually. Most organizations of this type provide their members with a printed synopsis of the proceedings of their conventions or seminars. Members who are inclined toward research share their discoveries with others through these publications, which often provide scholarly information that is available only in this one-time and very limited type of publication.

The areas of specialization in collecting have increased enormously in the past few years. Objects that are only a few decades old have piqued the interest of many new collectors. Dealers in specialized collectibles have increased in number and economic conditions have led to collectibles becoming second careers for many former collectors. They have watched objects they collected at the right time increase in value and the demand caused by a new generation of eager collectors has inspired them to sell what they own and search for other, similar items to supply their customers.

This is especially true in the more recent areas of collecting. People who once collected old railroad timetables, old cameras, objects made in Occupied Japan, or Walt Disney toys just for fun now find that there are many new collectors of the same things who are willing to pay what appear to the older hobbyist to be high prices for what they own. Many of the collector-dealers operate out of their homes, advertise in esoteric journals, and are relatively unknown outside of the circle of people who share their interests and special enthusiasms.

What is interesting and exciting to collect for some may often be an enigma to those outside of the collecting world. Today, objects of no real intrinsic beauty or value are treasured by specialist collectors. In addition, there are many new items being manufactured and hyped in the media as "instant" collector's items. The aspiring collector is often at a loss to decide what, of the many collecting areas, is a sound investment. He or she is, rightfully, concerned about spending money for new collector's series of plates, coins, thimbles, bells, or one of the many other newly made objects that have recently flooded the market.

If you are on the right computer list, hardly a day will go by when you are not offered through the mail a "once in a lifetime" opportunity to invest in a first-edition plate or some other item. From an investment point of view, these new collector's items are probably the most dangerous form of collecting and require very careful selection by the consumer who wants to see an appreciation in value over a period of time.

Most collectors find a specialty that has appeal to them because of nostalgia, historical interest, or some connection the objects they collect have to their occupation. They enjoy reading about and researching the crafts methods by which objects were made and know the political or social background that causes what they collect to be unique.

This book is written for those who are searching for a collecting field that has special meaning to them. Categories include a few of the old, established collecting areas as well as most of the newer fields where possibilities for seeing an increase in value over a period of time are good. Where they exist, clubs and specialized journals are listed, as well as source material for study. For those who own objects in the listed categories, the source material will put you in touch with collectors who might want to buy from you.

The law of "supply and demand" is as applicable to the collecting field as it is in any other area of commerce. It is up to you, as the seller or the buyer, to find out all you can about what you own or purchase before any transactions take place. Whether you collect for pleasure or for eventual financial return, you must know what you are doing. Those who collect are aware that they are taking risks, but if they collect wisely and knowledgeably, they have added a dimension to their lives that is as rewarding as the profit they or their heirs will someday realize when their collections are sold.

Choose a specialized area of collecting that appeals to you, read all you can about it, and talk to those who are already knowledgeable in that field. Whether your enthusiasm is for Mickey Mouse, Coca-Cola, or political buttons, there are many others who share that enthusiasm. Build your collection thoughtfully and carefully; get to know others who share your interests. Aside from the investment possibilities, collecting can add another dimension to your life and open opportunities for new interests and relationships.

There are many categories of collecting listed that have no books published about them, that are the focus for no journals or clubs. Many of these categories are relatively new and may be excellent investment areas for the beginning collector to consider. If you become interested and knowledgeable, you might be the one to write the first book.

PART I

BACKGROUND INFORMATION AND SOURCES

WHERE TO FIND
BOOKS ABOUT
COLLECTIBLES

It is necessary for every specialist collector to learn everything there is to know about an area of collecting before making an investment in specific items. There are dealers who specialize in collectors' books and sell them through the mail or at antique shows.

The leading dealers are:

R. J. Beck Company
Dept. E 2108
Hunter Street
Huntertown, Indiana 46748

Bethlehem Book Company
East Street
Bethlehem, Connecticut 06751
(Will send free list on request.)

Collector Books Clearing House
P. O. Box 3008
Paducah, Kentucky 42001
(Will send free book lists on request.)

The Collectors' Shelf of Books
23 Crandall Street, Box 6
Westfield, New York 14787
(Will send free catalog and price list.)

Edmonds Book Sales
P. O. Box 143-A
Ledbetter, Kentucky 42058

John Houghmaster
539 Second Avenue
North Troy, New York 12182
(No list, but will have or find for you any book on collecting, in or out of print. Write to ask what books they have on any collecting subject.)

The Reference Rack
P. O. Box 445K
Orefield, Pennsylvania 18069
(Will send free catalog and provide prompt service.)

GENERAL PERIODICALS ON ANTIQUES AND COLLECTIBLES

The following is a list of some of the general periodicals that are available for collectors. Most list coming sales and auctions and report on past sales. They carry dealer advertising and have articles of general interest to dealers and collectors. Write to find out current subscription rates. Some of them will send sample copies on request.

American Art & Antiques
One Worth Avenue
Marion, Ohio 43302

American Collector
13920 Mt. McClellan Blvd.
Reno, Nevada 89506

Antique Gazette
929 Davidson Drive
Nashville, Tennessee 37205

Antique Monthly
P. O. Box 2274
Birmingham, Alabama 35201

The Antique Trader Weekly
Dubuque, Iowa 52001

Antiques and the Arts Weekly
The Bee Publishing Company
Newtown, Connecticut 06470

Antiques Journal
Box 1046
Dubuque, Iowa 52001

Collectibles Monthly
P. O. Box 2023A
York, Pennsylvania 17405

The Collector
Drawer C
Kermit, Texas 79745

Joel Sater's Antiques & Auction News
Box B
Marietta, Pennsylvania 17547

The Magazine Antiques
551 Fifth Avenue
New York, New York 10017

Maine Antique Digest
Box 358F
Waldoboro, Maine 04572

*The New York Antique Almanac
  of Art, Antiques, Investments, &
  Yesteryear*
P. O. Box 335, Dept. 5
Lawrence, New York 11559

FLEA MARKETS AND OTHER SOURCES FOR BUYING COLLECTIBLES

All veteran collectors know that there are many sources for ferreting out objects that will add more prestige and importance to their collections. Specialist collectors know, also, that their best contacts are made through clubs and groups formed of people who collect similar items. A lot of trading goes on among club members at meetings, during shows, and through club bulletins and publications. Other mail sources are the advertisers in the more general publications for antiquers and popular collectibles buffs. Periodicals such as *Hobbies* and *Antiques, The Magazine,* as well as other publications mentioned in the previous chapter, are excellent sources for contact with general or specialist dealers.

Dedicated collectors who have the time and energy follow advertisements for local flea markets, house sales, and garage sales and are not discouraged if nine out of ten stops yield nothing that they want. There is always the chance that a treasure will be discovered that will turn out to be a bargain. As supplies of desirable collectibles become smaller, dealers and their suppliers also haunt house sales. The competition requires stamina and the ability to spot objects quickly.

Auctions, too, have become more competitive lately. Collectors compete with dealers in this arena, but dealers are wary about bidding higher than current wholesale value. The private collector can often outbid a dealer without paying the full retail price. If you enjoy auctions and can trust yourself not to be carried away by the excitement of the event, you can still find some good values in popular collector's items. There are a few rules to follow, however, if you are going to buy at auction. First, never bid on anything that you have not inspected carefully previous to the auction. Second, make a list of what you would like to bid on and note the absolute top price you are willing to pay. Third, never go above your projected top price; auctioneers can be hypnotic and persuasive. Fourth, bid only on objects that are familiar to you and about which you have knowledge. As good, genuine collectibles become more and more scarce, fakes and reproductions show up at auctions with some frequency and once you have made the top bid, the item is yours.

Thousands of local flea markets are held throughout the country, especially in the spring and summer. These outdoor marketplaces are often excellent sources for popular collector's items at favorable prices. The small flea markets are usually made up of part-time dealers, specialist collectors who want to sell duplicates, and people who rent space to sell objects they have gathered through a lifetime or have inherited. What is "junk" to them might be the treasure you have been searching for. These small markets are places where the collector may find an entire album of old greeting cards, picture postcards, old photographs, or trade cards.

There are also many established larger flea markets throughout the country that are open one or two days a week. There are few amateur dealers at these. Most people who rent space at these enterprises are established dealers who move some of their wares from shops to outdoor or indoor weekend marketplaces where they have more exposure and heavier traffic. It is at these markets that you will find dealers of popular collectibles such as Depression glass, carnival glass, limited edition plates, Occupied Japan objects, and many other categories that are not yet antique, but possibly desirable to many collectors. Among these, however, you will also find a lot of fakes and reproductions as well as some objects that have been broken and repaired. Dealers have to keep their tables or booths well stocked and there is no policing of quality or condition.

If you like the bazaar atmosphere of flea markets and enjoy the hunt, these huge marketplaces are fun to attend and there is always the chance of coming across the occasional bargain. The list below includes some of the larger flea markets across the country.

Antique and Collectibles Market
Wheaton, Illinois
(Third Sunday of the month)

Antique Show and Flea Market
4H Fairgrounds, Route 30
Amboy, Illinois
(Third Sunday monthly)

Canton First Monday Trades Day
Canton, Texas
(First Monday of the month)

Country Fair Antique Flea Market
2045 Dixie Highway
Pontiac, Michigan
(Friday, Saturday, Sunday)

Denver Antique Market
Denver, Colorado
(Weekends in the summer)

Englishtown Auction Sales
Englishtown, New Jersey
(Saturdays)

Georgia Antique Fair and Flea Market
Fairgrounds (Lakewood Park)
Atlanta, Georgia
(Second weekend each month)

Joplin Flea Market
1200 Block, Virginia Avenue
Joplin, Missouri
(Saturday and Sunday)

Knoxville Fairgrounds Flea Market
Knoxville, Tennessee
(Third weekend each month)

Paramount Flea Market
Paramount, California
(Sundays)

Renninger's Flea Market
Adamstown, Pennsylvania
(Saturdays)

Renninger's Flea Market
Kutztown, Pennsylvania
(Sundays)

Rose Bowl Flea Market
Pasadena, California
(Second Sunday each month)

San Jose Flea Market
San Jose, California
(Saturday and Sunday)

Shupp's Grove
Adamstown, Pennsylvania
(Saturday and Sunday)

Swap-O-Rama
Bakersfield, California
(Wednesday, Friday, Saturday, Sunday)

The Trading Post Center
451 West High Street
Elizabethtown, Pennsylvania
(Saturday and Sunday)

U. S. Route 1 Flea Market
New Brunswick, New Jersey
(Friday, Saturday, Sunday)

Woodbury Flea Market
Woodbury, Connecticut
(Saturday and Sunday in spring, summer, and fall)

The flea market events of the year are the three huge outdoor markets held one weekend each in May, July, and September in Brimfield, Massachusetts. This market attracts close to one thousand dealers from all over the country who come in vans, campers, and trucks and set up all day and night on Friday. They shop by flashlight from other dealers throughout the night. Although the market is advertised as "open to the public" on Saturday and Sunday, the collectors with stamina also arrive on Friday and shop along with the dealers. At Brimfield, you are apt to find antiques of great value, many early twentieth-century collectibles, and a lot of junk. The flea market, held on Auction Acres, a huge outdoor area, is set up on three predesignated weekends in May, July, and September. You can find out the exact dates by writing:

The Gordon Reid Company
Brimfield, Massachusetts 01010

Although the Reid Flea Market is the great draw, all of Brimfield celebrates these events and there are yard sales and tag sales along all routes leading into the town. Wear comfortable shoes and be prepared for changeable New England weather.

Antique shows usually offer higher quality merchandise than flea markets. The shows are held throughout the country in armories, indoor shopping malls, and other buildings capable of holding large crowds and many dealer displays. These are advertised in local newspapers and in most antiques journals and magazines. Specialists and general dealers rent spaces in these shows, which range from those featuring high quality art and antiques to shows limited to popular collector's items. Most of

these shows are annual events to which collectors look forward each year; they are held primarily from early fall through December. Some are two- or three-day events; the majority are one-week affairs.

Most collectors who specialize develop business relationships with dealers who also specialize. This is undoubtedly the easiest method of building a worthwhile collection. Find a dealer who keeps a list of your wants and who will notify you when those items turn up. There are dealers throughout the country who specialize in categories of collector's items, who are aware of the going prices for these items, and who are knowledgeable and fair. They will help you build your collection at a rate you can afford, will usually guarantee what they sell, and are often willing to buy back whatever they have sold you for at least what you paid. Dealers who specialize in one type of object are usually expert in their fields and treat their collectors fairly since they must depend on the collectors for repeat business. Published guides to regional antiques and collectibles dealers abound and can usually be found in your local library or bookstore.

Regardless of what route you decide to follow in buying additions to your collection, there is no substitute for knowledge. Read all books and journals pertaining to your particular interest in collecting. Learn to recognize marks, art styles, and methods of handcrafting and decorating. Attend shows of antiques or collectibles before you begin to make purchases; talk to dealers and collectors who have the special knowledge you will need to invest wisely. Join a club if one is available and subscribe to as many periodicals as you can afford and have the time to read. These will lead you to the right dealers, antiques shows, flea markets, and museum exhibits, where you can learn everything you need to know about investing wisely and building a meaningful, interesting collection that will reflect your taste and possibly increase in value with time. Most of the dealers listed in the next chapter will buy in their special categories as well as sell to you. If you are attempting to sell some treasures, write to them listing what you have, include a photograph and/or accurate description with measurements, marks, or other pertinent details and price wanted, and include a self-addressed, stamped envelope (SASE) for a prompt answer.

HOW TO FIND SPECIALIST DEALERS

There are thousands of dealers in antiques and popular collectibles. The majority of these do not have shops. Many display only at shows, while others sell only through the mail. Some, who specialize in one category of collectible, advertise in newsletters or club publications. Some of these dealers are collectors who use classified ads as a way of disposing of surplus collectibles to support their collecting habits.

Although the following is a list of dealers who specialize in the various categories of small collectibles discussed in this book, many will have items that are not within their major category. For instance, a dealer who advertises old sheet music will probably have other types of paper collectibles. Depression glass dealers often have other kinds of glass for sale. These same dealers are also a source for ceramics of the 1920s or 1930s and objects marked "Made in Occupied Japan." Send a description of your wants with a self-addressed, stamped envelope (SASE). They will let you know if they have what you want in stock; if not, they will try to get it for you.

When you establish a good relationship with the specialists, they will let you know when they are going to be in your area at shows and what they have found in your line of collecting, and they will help you build a collection that is worthwhile. Of course, all this takes time, patience, and trust between buyer and seller.

SOURCE LIST BY CATEGORY

Advertising

Stan Hecker
5010 Cadet Street
San Diego, California 92117
(For list send 50¢ and large SASE.)

Larry Shapiro
Box 101
Rocky Hill, Connecticut 06067

Muleskinner Antiques
10626 Main Street
Clarence, New York 14031

Akro Agate

Sophia Papapanau
141 Sedgwick Road
Syracuse, New York 13203

George and Roni Sionakides
6565 Herbison Road
DeWitt, Michigan 48820

Art Nouveau and Art Deco

All Accessories
P. O. Box 173
Ambler, Pennsylvania 19002

L'Imagerie
15030 Ventura Boulevard
Sherman Oaks, California 91403

The Jordan-Volpé Gallery
457 West Broadway
New York, New York 10012

D. Leonard and Gerry Trent
950 Madison Avenue
New York, New York 10021

Vintage Years Antiques
619 Palisade Avenue
Cliffside Park, New Jersey 07010

Banks
(Mechanical and Still)

F. H. Griffith
P. O. Box 323
Sea Girt, New Jersey 08750

Donald Markey
179 Palmers Hill Road
Stamford, Connecticut 06902

Barbershop Collectibles

Robert Doyle
98 Main Street
Fishkill, New York 12524
(Will send five catalogs, with more than
two hundred items in each, for $6.00.)

Sidney Penner
48 Paseo Laredo North
Cathedral City, California 92234

Beatrix Potter Characters

The Couchant Lion Antiques
Route 1, Box 296B
Oak Grove Road
Seaford, Delaware 19973
(Specializes in Vienna bronzes of Potter
characters.)

Breweriana

Oscar L. David
Box 24280
Los Angeles, California 90024
(Specializes in beer cans and other brew-
ery collectibles. Send $1.00 for list.)

Glentiques, Ltd.
P. O. Box 337
Glenford, New York 12433
(Specializes in collectible steins. Send
SASE for list.)

Pete's Beer Can Palace
1100 Chestnut Street
Ottawa, Illinois 61350

Bottles and Fruit Jars

Mary Bell Antiques
2405 South Main Street
Bloomington, Illinois 61701

Rene's Reliques
Route 1, Box 505
Gridley, California 95948

Trading Post Antiques
1045 Park Avenue
Chico, California 95926

Stamford Imports
P. O. Box 3807C
Stamford, Connecticut 06905

Dennis and Faith Wong
Flint Box 235
Fall River, Massachusetts 02723

Boxes

American Sampler
Box 432
Westwood, New Jersey 07675
(New Bilston and Battersea boxes. Send
$1.00 for catalog.)

Halcyon Days Ltd.
14 Brook Street
Hanover Square
London W1Y 1AA
England
(Upon request, will send catalog of
mostly new, some old, small enameled
boxes.)

John P. Schoenberg
2966 Roma Court
Santa Clara, California 95051

Carnival Glass

The Colechun Box
P. O. Box 26
Pyatt, Arkansas 72672

Marion T. Hartung
Box 69
Emporia, Kansas 66801

Pipedream Antiques
73 Wendell Road
Newton, Massachusetts 02159

Whitehouse Antiques and Collectibles
RD 1 Box 195
Dallastown, Pennsylvania 17313

Celebrity Collectibles

Chuck Ayers
P. O. Box 8059
Van Nuys, California 91409

Lorraine Burdick
5 Court Place
Puyellup, Washington 98371
(Film and theater material for collectors. Send 25¢ for list.)

Taimar Miles
3620 Holly Springs Drive
Forth Worth, Texas 76133
(Deals in movie posters, still publicity photos, etc.)

Cine Monde
1488 Vallejo Street
San Francisco, California 94109
(Features movie material.)

Bill Tucker
Rte. 6
Leslie, Arkansas 72645
(Mostly handles movie memorabilia.)

Coca-Cola Memorabilia

The Nostalgia Company
21 South Lake Drive
Hackensack, New Jersey 07601
(Send $2.00 for mail auction list.)

Cindy Rabb
Box 304
Newton Highland, Massachusetts 02161

The Real Thing
11702 Ventura Boulevard
Studio City, California 91604
(Send $1.75 for pocket price guide and list.)

John Stone
6810 Chambers Avenue
Cleveland, Ohio 44105

Thom Thompson
Huntertown Road
Versailles, Kentucky 40383

Comic Books

David Belcher
231 South Main Street
Orange, Massachusetts 01364
(Write listing your wants; include SASE.)

Daniels
229 Rumson Road, NE
Atlanta, Georgia 30305

Ron Haydon
250 Aqueduct Street
Welland, Ontario
Canada L3C 1C7
(Will send list.)

Commemorative China

William R. and Teresa F. Kurau
P. O. Box 406
Jackson Heights, New York 11372
(Send SASE for free list.)

Richard G. Marder
Box 6053
Harrisburg, Pennsylvania 17112

The Toby House
526 Danbury Road
Wilton, Connecticut 06897

Coronation China

British Collectibles, Ltd.
5613 Wilshire Boulevard
Los Angeles, California 90036

Country Store Collectibles

Ebenezer's Country Store
Box 172
Greendale, Massachusetts 01606

Walden Hill Country Store
Box 424
Wadsworth, Ohio 44281

Cut Glass

Raphael F. Borelli, Jr.
19 Buswell Avenue
Methuen, Massachusetts 01844

Cutter's Wheel Antiques
P. O. Box 285
Webster, New York 14580

Depression Glass

Barbara Cooper's Depression Shop
97 Weaver Street
Montgomery, New York 12549

Gloria's Antiques
1514 East Southmore Street
Pasadena, Texas 77502

Iris's Depression Glass
Iris Slayton
3250 Allison and 3rd Street
Groves, Texas 77619

Madge and Ruth Kelley
P. O. Box 117, RR 4
Princeton, Illinois 61356

Margaret Knowles
Frankfort, Maine 04438

Betty Newbound
4567 Chadsworth Street
Union Lake, Michigan 48085

Greenwich Gallery
38 West Putnam Avenue
Greenwich, Connecticut 06830

Reid's
P. O. Box 645
Edmonds, Washington 98020

Sentimental Journey Antiques
P. O. Box 82
Park Ridge, Illinois 60068

Tom's Treasure House
Thomas F. Duncan
1288 Oakdale Road, NE
Atlanta, Georgia 30307

Victorian Manor
20 South Eastern Avenue
Joliet, Illinois 60433

Roserita Ziegler
174 South Mountain Road
New Britain, Connecticut 06052

Dolls

Antique Dolls Unlimited
2318 St. Charles Avenue
New Orleans, Louisiana 70130
(Send 50¢ and two first-class stamps for list.)

Melton's Antiques
4201 Indian River Road
Chesapeake, Virginia 23325
(Send SASE for free list.)

Arlene Schutz
P. O. Box 363
Washington, Missouri 63090

Regina A. Stuli
23 Wheatfield Drive
Wilmington, Delaware 19810
(Send 50¢ and SASE for list.)

Fiesta Ware

Fiesta Finders
112 Williamsburg Circle
Monroe, Louisiana 71203

Don Wiggins
Box 228
Clemson, South Carolina 29631

Heisey, Cambridge, Duncan Miller Glass

Last Chance Antiques
60 North Federal Highway
Dania, Florida 33004

Mostly Heisey
Rhoda Curely
16 Clayton Place
Albany, New York 12209

C. Young
12823 Wenlock Street
St. Louis, Missouri 63141

Roserita Ziegler
174 South Mountain Road
New Britain, Connecticut 06052

Hummels

The Assemblage
P. O. Box 259
Inwood Station
New York, New York 10034

Eileen Grande
12 Iroquois Avenue
Saratoga Springs, New York 12866

Hildegarde's
C-597 Farmington Avenue
Hartford, Connecticut 06105

L. P. Keely
Box F
Delray Beach, Florida 33444

Indian Art (American)

Capistrano Trading Post
31741 Camino Capistrano
San Juan Capistrano, California 92675

Hastings House
Essex Square
Essex, Connecticut 06426

Just Us
J. & S. Schneider
299 Court Avenue
Tucson, Arizona 85701

Native American Art
949 Walnut Street
Boulder, Colorado 80302

Pueblo One Indian Arts
3815 North Brown Avenue
Scottsdale, Arizona 85251

Bob Ward
201–203 West San Francisco Street
Santa Fe, New Mexico 87501

Insulators

L. Doe
Box 445
Woodlake, California 93286
(Send 10¢ plus SASE for price list.)

Kitchen Collectibles

Bob's Place
Box 283
Clinton, Iowa 52732
(Send $1.00 for list, refundable on first order.)

The Cunninghams
P. O. Box 142
Denver, Pennsylvania 17517

Hobart House
Box 128
Haddam, Connecticut 06438

Limited Edition Collector's Plates

A. G. Beebe
12918 Harney Street
Omaha, Nebraska 68154

Calhoun's Collector's Society, Inc.
Calhoun Center
7275 Bush Lake Road
Minneapolis, Minnesota 55435

Hollywood Limited Editions, Inc.
6990 North Central Park
Lincolnwood, Illinois 60645

Maurice Nasser
New London Shopping Center
New London, Connecticut 06320

Matchbook Covers

Myers
Box 425
Trolley Station
Detroit, Michigan 48231
(Send 50¢ for list.)

Miniatures and Dollhouses

Chestnut Hill Studio
Box 907
Taylors, South Carolina 29687
(Catalog price is $3.00, 50¢ of which is
refundable on first order.)

Don Cnossen
P. O. Box 7514
St. Petersburg, Florida 33703
(Specializes in handcrafted colonial mini-
atures, including Shaker items. Send
SASE for list.)

G. Freund
Box 160532
Miami, Florida 33116
(Has miniatures and dollhouse kits. Cat-
alog price is $2.00, refundable with
first $10.00 order.)

Mini Mania
28 Sherwood Place
Greenwich, Connecticut 06830

The Penney Doll
100 Main Street
North Woodbury, Connecticut 06798

Needlework and Sewing Devices

Frantiques
Kellyville RFD 1, Box 287
Claremont, New Hampshire 03743
(Send SASE for list.)

Theresa and Arthur Greenblatt
Amherst, New Hampshire 03031

Julie and Craig Coste
96 Broad Street
Plattsburgh, New York 12901

Thomas K. Woodard
1022 Lexington Avenue
New York, New York 10021
(Specializes in textiles and quilts.)

Occult

Back East Antiques
P. O. Box 4689
Glendale, California 91202
(Offers Masonic items.)

Magickal Childe
Abrahadabra, Inc.
37 West 19th Street
New York, New York 10011
(Send $2.00 for catalog of new items.)

Sallie's Specialties
Box 7732
Atlanta, Georgia 30357
(Features Tarot cards.)

Occupied Japan Collectibles

Antiquities at Large
Box 3016
Farmington, New Mexico 87401
(Send $1.00 for list.)

Chelouise Antiques
1818 Highland Road
Baton Rouge, Louisiana 70802

Fenner's Antiques
2611 Avenue S
Brooklyn, New York 11229
(Send 50¢ for list.)

Arline V. Wise
Route 1
Athol, Massachusetts 01331

Paper Dolls

Barbara Bisgaard
Route 2
DeKalb, Illinois 60115
(Send long SASE for list.)

Paperweights

Gems in Glass
Box 542
Woodbridge, New Jersey 07055
(Send $1.00 and SASE for list.)

Theresa and Arthur Greenblatt
Amherst, New Hampshire 03031

Leo Kaplan Antiques
910 Madison Avenue
New York, New York 10021

Sevenoaks Antiques
Box 280 Kingsbridge Station
Riverdale, New York 10463

Photographica
(Equipment and Images)

Joe Buberger
P. O. Box 211
North Haven, Connecticut 06473

Janet Lehr
Box 617
New York, New York 10028

Neikrug Galleries, Inc.
224 East 68th Street
New York, New York 10021

Allen and Hilary Weiner
80 Central Park West
New York, New York 10023

Political Items

Chuck Ayers
P. O. Box 8059
Van Nuys, California 91409

Dave Beck
Mediapolis, Iowa 52637
(Send $1.00 for list.)

Max Kaplan
Box 1674
Carlsbad, California 92008
(Specializes in Kennedy memorabilia.)

Political Americana
Box 21
Closter, New Jersey 07624
(Send 50¢ for illustrated catalog.)

James Tyler
511 Chester Avenue
Clifton Heights, Pennsylvania 19018

Postcards

Alan's Alley
79-A Watchung Avenue
North Plainfield, New Jersey 07060
(Send a list of your wants and a SASE.)

V. G. Block
Long Pond, Pennsylvania 18334
(List your wants and include a SASE.)

Sally Carver
179 South Street
Chestnut Hill, Massachusetts 02167
(Conducts auctions by mail. Send a
    SASE.)

W. LaVenture
19251 Brookhurst Street
Huntington Beach, California 92646
(Sends free lists.)

Don Preziosi
275 Water Street
New York, New York 10038

Railroadiana

Fred Arone
377 Ashford Avenue
Dobbs Ferry, New York 10522

Miller
3106 North Rochester Street
Arlington, Virginia 22213

T & L Railroad
4512 Montrose Street
Houston, Texas 77006

Schoolhouse Collectibles

The Black Stove Shop
Ray and Candy Manocchio
Route 201
Riverside Drive
Augusta, Maine 04330

Mort Packman
8113 Crittendon Street
Philadelphia, Pennsylvania 19118
(Deals in old schoolbooks. Send a SASE
   for lists.)

Sheet Music

Robert Greenlaw
307 North Rampart Street, Room 442
Los Angeles, California 90026

McCall
50 Grove Street
New York, New York 10014
(Send $3.00 for catalog.)

McNeil
1117 South Taylor Street
Oak Park, Illinois 60304
(Send 65¢ for first list; lists are free
   thereafter.)

Plantation Galleries
3750 Government Boulevard
Mobile, Alabama 36609
(Send 50¢ for list.)

Silver

Antique Silver, Ltd.
P. O. Box 3243
Cherry Hill, New Jersey 08034

Silver Antiquities
P. O. Box 7092
Kansas City, Missouri 64113
(Send $1.00 for list.)

The Spoon Rack
7 Colrain Road
Topsfield, Massachusetts 01983

Soapstone Carvings

Greenwich Gallery
38 West Putnam Avenue
Greenwich, Connecticut 06830

Sports Memorabilia

Julie and Craig Coste
96 Broad Street
Plattsburgh, New York 12901

The Paper Chase
112 East Ponce de Leon Avenue
Decatur, Georgia 30030

Bob Walter
Box 7
Westport, Connecticut 06880

Tools

Keith Parker
Box 66
111 West 13th Street
Kewanee, Illinois 61443
(Send $1.00 for an illustrated list.)

Toys and Games

Charlie's Toy Chest
2829 Bird Avenue
Miami, Florida 33133

Ralph Gries
3351 North Holton Street
Milwaukee, Wisconsin 53212

S. Leonard
P. O. Box 127
Albertson, New York 11507
(Send 50¢ and a SASE for list.)

Mouse House Farm Antiques
Ada M. and Walter B. Slifer
P. O. Box 276
Yarmouth Port, Massachusetts 02675

Trade Cards

The Glass Bottle
Box 374
Sutter Creek, California 95685

Loccisano
216 Foal Court
Lancaster, Pennsylvania 17602

Dorothy Wilkison
P. O. Box 251
Bradenton, Florida 33305
(Send 50¢ and a SASE for list.)

Wedgwood

The Antiques Market
Marian and Aaron Levine
881 Whalley Avenue
New Haven, Connecticut 06515

E. Richardson
140 South Broadway
North Attleboro, Massachusetts 02760

Seal Simons
473 West Ellet Street
Philadelphia, Pennsylvania 19119

Leslie F. Slavid & Sons
552 Washington Street
Wellesley, Massachusetts 02181

World's Fairs
and Expositions

Ortte
1436 Killarney Street
Los Angeles, California 90065
(Send SASE for Expo Collector's Club
   information.)

THE MATCHMAKERS

There was a time, not too many years ago, when a part dinner set could be bought at country auctions in a box lot for a few dollars. At auctions of this type, you might also be able to purchase a group of sterling or silverplate flatware that could be made up into four or five place settings in a pattern that was discontinued a generation or two ago.

These bargains can seldom be found today, but there are many people who inherit part sets of flatware or dishes in a pattern they like. Part sets of anything are of little use, but there are dealers throughout the country who specialize in matching your mother's or grandmother's china and silver. With patience and a nominal investment, depending on the quality and age of what you want to match, you can complete many of the discontinued patterns in Haviland, Wedgwood, Lenox, or other dinnerware. There are dealers who will find you the missing forks, knives, or spoons that will fill in a sterling or silverplate pattern until you have the desired number of place settings. Send them a description of your wants with a stamped and self-addressed envelope (SASE) and they will let you know what they have in stock or will find what you want from their files.

SILVER MATCHING SERVICES

Mrs. Tere Hagan
Box 3132
Thousand Oaks, California 91359

House of Antiques
202 North 5th Street
Springfield, Illinois 62701

Marleda's
Box 2308, Dept. 25
San Bernardino, California 92406
(Specializes in silverplate. Send a long
  SASE for list.)

Toby's Antiques
Route 1, Box 547
Odessa, Texas 79763

CHINA MATCHING SERVICES

The Blue Plate Antiques
P. O. Box 121
Sherborn, Massachusetts 01770
(Specializes in matching Flow Blue and
  Mulberry china. Send a SASE with in-
  quiry.)

The China Match
9 Elmsford Road
Rochester, New York 14606
(Matches Syracuse patterns and others.
  List your wants in your first letter and
  include a SASE.)

Rosemary Evans
9303 McKinney Street
Loveland, Ohio 45140
(Matches Wedgwood patterns. Send a
  SASE with your inquiry.)

Gusers
Route 1, Box 426
Rolla, Missouri 65401
(Matches cups to saucers or vice versa in
  English china only.)

Barbara W. Hite
120 Wildwood Lane
Anchorage, Kentucky 40223
(Specializes in Haviland china. Indicate your wants and supply a SASE.)

Jacquelynn's China
4124 North Maryland Avenue
Milwaukee, Wisconsin 53211
(Specializes in matching Lenox patterns.)

Laura's Antiques and Gifts
2625 West Britton Road
Oklahoma City, Oklahoma 23120
(China and crystal replacement center. Send request with SASE.)

Vera L. Phillips
6427 South Prince Street
Littleton, Colorado 81120
(Matches Haviland china; send SASE with request.)

Robinson
517 North Pennsylvania Avenue
Morrisville, Pennsylvania 19067
(Matches Lenox patterns.)

Vintage Patterns II
5304 Thrasher Drive
Cincinnati, Ohio 45239
(Matches Noritake patterns.)

The Wedgwood China Cupboard
740 North Honey Creek Parkway
Milwaukee, Wisconsin 53213
(Matches Wedgwood china and pottery tableware.)

White's
P. O. Box 680
Newburg, Oregon 97132
(Supplies replacements for Lenox and Spode patterns.)

DO-IT-YOURSELF REPAIRS, MATERIALS, AND PARTS

All collectibles and antiques are subject to breakage, wear, and aging, no matter what materials they are made of. This chapter offers some suggestions for those who would like to attempt repairs themselves. For very valuable items, you will want professional help and should consult the following chapter.

BARBERSHOP COLLECTIBLES

If your favorite collectible is barbershop memorabilia, you can write for a free parts listing for barber poles to:

Wm. Marvy Company
1538 St. Clair Avenue
St. Paul, Minnesota 55105

Also included will be a special free publication, "Origin of the Barber Pole."

DOLLS

Restoration of old dolls requires some talent with needle and thread, knowledge of period styles of dress, and the patience to search out textiles and trim appropriate to that style. It also necessitates information on where to find parts of dolls' bodies or facial features that might be broken or missing. An excellent source for purchasing dolls' wigs, hand-sewn bodies, reproduction china and bisque parts, leather handmade shoes, blown glass eyes, and even dolls' eyelashes is:

Dollspart Supply Company
46-13 11th Street
Long Island City, New York 11101

Request a free catalog.

HARDWARE

Replicas of stamped brass hardware for furniture and other old items are available from:

Ritter and Son Hardware
Dept. 601
Gualala, California 95445

This company's catalog costs $1.00 and they also sell an antiquing solution to age any new brass parts.

While Ritter's hardware is mostly nineteenth-century style, earlier brass reproduction furniture hardware is available from another source:

Horton Brasses
Nooks Hill Road
P. O. Box 95-N
Cromwell, Connecticut 06416
(203-635-4400)

Horton's catalog costs $1.50 and includes

seventeenth-, eighteenth-, nineteenth-, and early twentieth-century pulls for drawers.

HOUSE RESTORATION

If you are not only a collector, but are in the process of restoring an entire house, or even if you are just thinking of it, the source book you can't do without is:

The 1980 Old-House Journal Catalog
69A Seventh Avenue
Brooklyn, New York 11217

This catalog tells you where to go to find anything you might want or need for authentic restoration from a tin ceiling to wide-plank flooring. The price, postpaid, is $8.95.

LAMPSHADES AND FIXTURES

Shades for old lamps and gas and electric fixtures can be purchased from:

Campbell Lamps
1108 Pottsdown Pike
West Chester, Pennsylvania 19380 (Dept. 11)

Send 60¢ for their catalog.

PAPER

Old paper items need special care if they are to last. All collectibles should be purchased in as good condition as possible, but it is incumbent on any collector to preserve that condition. Old sheet music, greeting cards, and picture postcards that are soiled or torn can be cleaned and repaired without detracting from their initial value.

Surface dirt on old paper items can be removed to some extent by rubbing soiled areas gently with an art gum eraser.

Small tears can also be repaired at home. If the tears are old they might require some cleaning before they are fixed. Lay torn edges on a clean, flat surface. Lifting one edge gently with a pair of tweezers, care-fully brush the other toward the tear, using a soft-bristled brush soaked in clear, warm water. Do the same with the other side. This will help eliminate a dirty line that might be visible after the tear has been repaired.

A paper item such as a piece of old sheet music or a picture postcard can be cleaned further by laying the print in a large, flat pan, such as those used for washing photographic prints, and running clear, warm water into the pan for five or ten minutes. The print can then be removed and blotted. The damp paper item is then placed between two pieces of blotting paper, clamped together sandwich-fashion between two pieces of plywood, and left until thoroughly dry. Drying may take several days.

Once the paper is dry, tears may be repaired by cutting a piece of rice paper to fit over the tear. Use only as much paper as is necessary to cover and reinforce the torn area. Wheat paste should be used as a gluing agent, since it will not pucker when dry. If the tear is a small one, brush paste on the edges of the tear and, using a clean, dry brush, work the feathered edges together. The rice paper can then be glued to the back to reinforce the tear.

Not all paper items are repairable by the above method. Only early lithographed sheet music printed on heavy rag paper can be soaked. Later sheet music was printed on inexpensive stock and will disintegrate in water. Lithographed picture postcards can be soaked for cleaning; newer (after around 1915) postcards cannot. The same is true of greeting cards.

Postcards and greeting cards of the last century or the first decade of this one were frequently pasted into albums. Many sets of trade cards were treated this way as well. Often the album pages have become brittle and rotted. Soaking by the method described above will usually separate the cards from the album pages. The glue can usually be rubbed off with your fingers while it is still wet. Dry the cards by the above process.

PORCELAIN, POTTERY, OR GLASS

If you collect valuable old porcelain, pottery, or glass, you have probably experienced a mishap or two resulting in the breakage of a favorite plate, figurine, or other object. These things can be mended, although they will never be worth their original value, nor will they be as easy to sell as they would be if they were still in mint condition. It is worthwhile to repair these items if the damage is not too severe, since they can still be used as cabinet pieces.

Whether you repair a broken piece of porcelain or glass yourself or have the work done by a professional will depend on the rarity and value of the piece and whether it is worth spending more money on making the object whole again. If it is not very valuable to start with, you might want to repair it yourself to keep the pieces together and to use it as a display piece. Most pottery, glass, or porcelain pieces will hold together with Elmer's Glue. This is for temporary repair only; if you wash the piece, it will once again come apart in your hands. A more permanent home repair can be made with one of the new, more durable glues such as Super Glue 3 made by Loctite. Use this glue according to the directions and take special care to work quickly. It should be used very sparingly and must be applied to one small surface at a time, since it dries very quickly. This glue is washable when dry, is almost invisible, and is especially useful for repairing glass objects.

If you are more ambitious and have more than one or two objects in pottery, glass, or porcelain that need mending, there are kits available for this purpose. Among these is a Master Mending Kit for glass and china. It includes five basic systems to rejoin and remold broken and missing pieces and to restore finishes and glazes. The kit includes step-by-step instructions, but it would be wise to practice on several objects of little value before you work on something you treasure. The kit is $14.95 and may be ordered from:

Atlas Minerals & Chemicals Division
EBS Incorporated
Mertztown, Pennsylvania 19539

Included in the Master Mending Kit are: Porcelainate for mending china and porcelain; Epoxyglass for mending glass; Epoxybond putty for mending pottery; porcelainizing finish with tints for coloring the mended seams without firing; Gloss Glaze for restoring glaze without firing.

Another home repair kit, for broken porcelain only, includes porcelain adhesive, porcelain base crack filler, finish porcelain crack filler, sandpaper, paint, and finish glaze. Instructions are, of course, included. This kit costs $15.00 (plus $2.00 handling and mailing charges) and can be ordered from:

Restorers of America
126 Main Street
Ravenna, New York 12143

Rim chips on glass objects can be repaired and, if they are not too deep, a useless object can be returned to usable condition. Small flakes on glass rims can be sandpapered smooth. For larger chips, take the vase, tumbler, or other object to a glassmaker for an estimate.

General do's and don'ts of care and repair are:

Don't wash any overglaze-decorated porcelain or pottery in strong detergent. Use warm water and mild soapsuds, rinse in clear warm water, and dry immediately. Never put any glass or china made before 1940 in the dishwasher.

Don't ever wash any American Indian pottery, and don't use these pots as flower vases. Most are very porous and were made as decorative items only. Water will cause them to crack and washing is apt to remove decoration.

Most porcelain and pottery marked Made in Occupied Japan is water-safe. However, a few types of figurines and other objects were overglaze-painted and tend to flake or chip. Dust with a soft brush only.

SILVER

Use good quality polish on your silver and do not put antique or new silver in the dishwasher.

TEXTILES

Most textile repairs can be done by anyone handy with needle and thread. Doll clothing, old stuffed toys, and other types of collectibles that are made of cloth usually cannot be harmed by home repairs. Museum-quality textiles should be cleaned and repaired by experts who specialize in this type of work. You will have to be the one to judge whether to try it yourself or to pay to have someone else do restoration for you. A recommendation on obtaining expert repairs is included in the next chapter.

TRUNKS

You can restore or repair old trunks by following instructions in the *Trunk Repair Book,* available from:

Antique Trunk Company
3706 West 169th Street
Cleveland, Ohio 44111

The book ($2.00 plus 35¢ postage) has 24 pages of instructions and you will get a parts catalog along with it.

WOOD

There are few restorations to small wood collectibles that cannot be done by anyone who has had some experience in a basement workshop. Surface dirt can be removed by a damp cloth and hard rubbing. For initial cleaning and restoration of wood grain and color, Goddard's Cabinet Makers Cream, applied according to directions on the can, is a safe and effective product. It can be used on leather as well as wood and it is especially good for lacquered pieces. It will remove fingermarks and dust from lacquered boxes and is safe for most decoration used on these boxes. If you have any qualms about using this polish, first try it on a small section. Goddard's Cabinet Makers Cream can be purchased in many hardware stores. If you have a difficult time finding it, write to:

J. Goddard & Sons
299 Madison Avenue
New York, New York 10017

An application of a good quality paste wax and further rubbing will bring out wood grain and restore the patina. Joints can be reglued by using any of the wood glue products presently on the market and following their instructions. For more complicated restoration of wood antiques or collectibles, call or write:

Old Mill Woodworks
Old Mill Road
Georgetown, Connecticut 06829
(203-544-8294)

Unless you are an expert on wood, don't let water come in contact with any box or other object that is inlaid or veneered.

Don't use water on any lacquered surface. Russian lacquer boxes with hand-painted decoration should be kept away from direct sunlight and radiators. They should be handled as little as possible.

PROFESSIONAL REPAIRS AND RESTORATION

If you are insecure about attempting repairs and restoration yourself or if your collectibles are too valuable for a home repair, there are many people who are professional restorers for objects made of special materials. Prices, of course, will vary according to the amount of restoration necessary. Unfortunately, the quality of work varies, too. If you plan to use a local person it is a good idea to ask other collectors or dealers in your area whom they use or recommend. If not, it would be worth getting estimates from the established craftspeople listed in this chapter.

Art objects and small antiques made of porcelain, pottery, wood, bronze, and other metals can be professionally restored; missing parts can be rebuilt, and breaks mended. Send your broken pieces to:

Rosti Studios
Brewster Hill Road
Brewster, New York 10509

They will mail you a detailed estimate for approval before they do any work on your object.

DOLLS

If you are not handy and have a doll that requires some repairs, look up "Dolls—Repairing" in your Yellow Pages. Professional doll restoration is done by:

The Doll Place
P. O. Box 536 Van Brunt Station
Brooklyn, New York 11215

Send a self-addressed, stamped envelope and a dime to them for a list of services offered for restoration and conservation of dolls.

GLASS

Objects made of stained glass can be repaired professionally by:

The Condon Studios
33 Richdale Avenue
Cambridge, Massachusetts 02140

Paperweight repair requires a specialist. Send your fractured, chipped, or scratched weight to:

Studio Hannah
Star Route A, Box 93
Flemington, New Jersey 08822

METALS

Repairs and restoration can be made to metal antiques and collectibles; if they are done right, the repairs do not detract from the intrinsic value of the object. Again, if your investment in the piece needing mending is large to begin with, it is worth having it restored properly. If you have a joint that needs soldering, this is a small job that can be done by anyone with the proper tools and materials. Look in your Yellow Pages. If you need quality restoration, call

Bill Vishnosky
Ridgefield, Connecticut 06877
(203-438-3695)

for an estimate. He mends anything in copper, brass, steel, or other metal and works mostly on antique restoration. Iron toy repairing is done by:

Russ Harrington
1805 Wilson Point Road
Baltimore, Maryland 21220

Old tin and copper objects in need of restoration require the understanding attention of people who know enough not to remove the patina on an old and valuable weather vane or to pound out the small dents and scars that show many years of service on copper or brass utensils. You can trust your metal collectibles to:

Inman's Tin & Coppersmithing
Star Route 2
Charleston, New Hampshire 03603
(603-542-0257)

Inman's also does gold leafing and can replace missing parts. Write to them and tell them what restoration is needed. Include, if possible, a photograph of the object you want restored or repaired and a self-addressed, stamped envelope.

TEXTILES

Museum-quality textiles should be cleaned and repaired by experts who specialize in this type of work. You will have to be the one to judge whether to try it yourself or pay to have someone else do restoration for you. Expert restoration of antique garments and textiles is done by:

Helene Von Rosenstiel
88 Prospect Park West
Brooklyn, New York 11215
(212-788-7909)

PACKING AND SHIPPING COLLECTIBLES

A lot of buying and selling goes on over the phone between dealers and collectors of antiques and collectible items. These objects frequently are mailed or shipped. Perhaps one of the reasons why stamps, coins, and paper collectibles are so popular is that the concern about breakage in shipping is negligible for these collecting areas. If you do collect in one of the categories of breakable items, there are things you should know about packing and shipping before you entrust a glass or ceramic treasure to the U. S. Postal Service or United Parcel.

PACKING

When you pack a small, breakable object, picture it placed on the bottom of a large truck with everyone else's package stacked on top of it. Imagine it being thrown from the truck to the sidewalk. Your package must be able to withstand this kind of treatment. Therefore, you must select packing materials very carefully and take the time to wrap and box your object so that it will have a chance of arriving safely. If you ship only a few packages a year, it won't pay you to purchase packing materials in quantity. Save padded paper, bubble wrap, Styrofoam chips, or other packing materials for the time when you might need them. If you don't have anything that will absorb shock when wrapped around a breakable object, the least expensive and most easily obtainable material to use for this purpose is disposable diapers. "Pampers" are the preferred brand for this purpose because they

are not contoured and you get more surface padding for your money. Wrap the Pampers around the object and tape them to hold. Use several layers and stuff any openings with more of the padding.

Place the object in a box that is just large enough to hold the wrapped piece. If the box is too large, stuff it with more crumpled paper or Pampers until there is no movement of the object when you shake the box. Tape this box shut. Put a layer of Styrofoam chips or any other shock-absorbing material on the bottom of a larger box and place the smaller box in the center of the larger box. Stuff more chips around the sides and sprinkle some across the top of the larger box before you tape that closed.

The outer box should be of strong material so that it can absorb a lot of weight. Two types of boxes that can be obtained free are suitable for this purpose. Banana boxes and tomato cartons are made of heavy, strong cardboard with removable lids. Both types can be obtained at your local supermarket or fruit and vegetable wholesaler. Ask the store manager when the boxes might be available and ask permission to take them.

If you use this box-within-a-box method for packing small breakables, there is a fairly good chance that your package will arrive safely. If you intend to do a reasonable amount of trading through the mail or United Parcel Service, you might want to invest in *Bubble Pak,* a double plastic wrap with entrapped air bubbles. This wrap is effective for protecting any fragile object for shipping. One 175-foot roll, perforated every 12 inches for tearing, costs $23 and can be ordered from:

Jonal
P. O. Box 102H
Scarsdale, New York 10583
(914-725-0012)

SHIPPING

There are two major carriers for packages. The one preferred is United Parcel Service (UPS), but this service is only available for packages that fall within the size range set up by them. A few years ago, this service was only available to businesses under contract to UPS, but it is now available to anyone who lives with a reasonable distance of a United Parcel depot. Check the White Pages of your local phone book; you will probably find a toll-free number to call for information concerning the closest depot. You must take your parcel to the depot for shipment. Unless you are under contract with them, UPS does not pick up.

UPS does not appear to go out of its way to solicit private business and is not listed under "Delivery Service" in the Yellow Pages. However, any local storekeeper can tell you where your closest depot is located.

In order to have your parcel accepted by UPS you must follow certain rules. For the lowest rate, a package should not be more than 108 combined inches (girth plus length). All packages must be wrapped or boxed carefully and secured with reinforced tape; no string is allowed. Each package is automatically insured up to $100 with a charge of 25¢ for each additional $100 insurance. No individual can ship more than 100 pounds to a single destination in one day. If a package is oversize, no matter how light it is, there is a minimum charge of the rate for 25 pounds. Each package must have a clearly printed address label which includes the zip code. United Parcel will deliver your package within a week to any destination in the continental United States. Rates depend on weight, size, and distance, but UPS is presently less expensive than Parcel Post. United Parcel Service also has an air service with a guaranteed two-day delivery time. This service is limited by UPS to items valued at $1,000 or less; destinations include Hawaii and Alaska.

If you live too far from the nearest UPS depot, you can use Parcel Post. However, the maximum weight accepted for packages sent between first class post offices is 40 pounds. The combined size (girth plus length) accepted is 100 inches. The maximum amount of insurance given is $400 and the cost for this is presently $2.75 for $300 to $400.

Wrapping and labeling instructions for Parcel Post are now the same as those at UPS. At one time, Parcel Post insisted on packages that could be opened for inspection and this precluded the use of tape closures.

DISPLAYING YOUR COLLECTION

Improper display of some types of collectibles can lead to damage or breakage, while the right use of display materials can enhance the beauty of whatever you collect. Whether you collect thimbles, limited edition plates, spoons, dolls, picture postcards, weather vanes, sheet music, miniatures, or any other of the many categories discussed in this book, there are materials and methods for display and storage that will keep them together, show them off to better advantage, and give them decorative importance in a room.

Weather vanes, for instance, become indoor sculpture when mounted on a plinth and look especially attractive when lighted with a strategically placed small spotlight. The right size heavy wooden block can be cut at your local lumberyard and painted a matte black. Make certain the balance is right so that the vane will not tip easily.

PLATES

Most limited edition plates are really wall plaques, designed by the artist to be hung rather than displayed flat. Most are decorated with designs that have a top and bottom. Like any painting or print, often collector's plates look better with some sort of frame. This is especially true when there is no self-framing border pattern. If your series of plates *is* designed with a border, all you need for hanging is a double-spring brass plate hanger. These hangers allow the plate to hang flat against the wall so that the design does not appear distorted. Only four tiny brass prongs will show in the front. The hangers are designed to hold plates that are 4", 5", 6", 7", 9", and 11" in diameter.

If you have never used a brass plate hanger, you should practice attaching one to a plate that has little value. It is easy to chip a rim if you are not very careful. Measure the plates you want to hang before you order the hangers, since any attempt to use the wrong size hanger may result in chipping or breaking.

Brass easels are another method for displaying collector's plates. These are made of twisted wire and will hold a plate upright on a table, mantel, or shelf. The easels come in a variety of sizes and can also be used for displaying framed picture postcards, old framed photographs, or any other small framed collectibles. Adjustable brass stands for centerpiece bowls and twisted brass wire cup-and-saucer easels are also available.

All of the above display materials are sold through a catalog issued free by:

T & B Sales
Box 30, Dept. AJ
Old Hickory, Tennessee 37138

Wood plate holders, rosewood stands, and legged stands in Chinese style can be purchased in sizes ranging from one to ten inches for round stands and three to ten inches for plate holders. These display pieces are more decorative than the brass stands and somewhat more expensive. They are attractive shelf, mantel, and table accessories that show off your porcelain, pottery, and glass collectibles. When ordering plate stands, the stand should be 20 per cent larger than the plate to be displayed. For information on what is available and prices on these wood items, write to:

Gimone
P. O. Box 637
Lenox Hill Station
New York, New York 10021

Plate frames, shadow boxes, shelves, thimble holders, spoon holders, display stands, display domes (bell jars), and other accessories for the collector are featured in a catalog sold for $1.00 (refundable on your first order) by:

M & R Specialties
P. O. Box 284, Dept. J
Worth, Illinois 60482

DOLLS

Doll stands are indispensable items for the collector who wants to show off free-standing dolls either singly or grouped together. Adjustable stands made of steel are available in the free catalog you can get by writing to:

Dollspart Supply Company
46-13 11th Street
Long Island City, New York 11101

PAPER

The proper display of paper collectibles requires special knowledge and materials. Old sheet music, picture postcards, posters, and prints can all be framed for display and make colorful and interesting accessories for a room. Whether you frame these items yourself or have the work done professionally, care must be taken that the paper items are framed in such a way that their value as collector's items will not be impaired. All old paper items should be backed and matted with acid-free ragboard. This will prevent deterioration and foxing (brown spots). Once started, this deterio-

ration is difficult to remove. Ragboard or even a textile backing is necessary. The ragboard can be purchased at most art supply stores.

If you have the inclination for framing your own paper collectibles, access to materials and tools, as well as instruction on how to use them, is available at many franchised frame shops across the country. People are encouraged to come in, use the tools—such as matte cutters, paper cutters, glass cutters, and other items that make framing easy—and learn to select framing materials that are complimentary to the object being framed. These shops have a wide variety of molding, backing, and matting material that will give you a large choice of combinations to set off your paper collectibles to the best advantage.

If you are willing to take the time to learn this craft, there are well-trained people who will teach you and you can save a lot of money if you have many items to frame. One of the franchised chains that has this service is called The Frame Shop. Most are in or near heavily populated areas.

When attaching paper items to a backing for framing, always use stamp hinges rather than glue. Never let anyone convince you that your paper collectible should be dry-mounted. This process might make your old poster or document appear more attractive when framed, but the object can never be separated from the backing and dry-mounting detracts from the intrinsic value of the item.

Small paper items with similar design and color value look more important when framed in groups of two, four, or six. Postcards by the same artist or of similar type can be mounted on a fabric background or matted in a colored cardboard that will pull the cards together as a unit.

All old paper collectibles, if framed, should be hung on a wall where the sun will not fade them. This is especially important for old documents or items with applied fabric such as woven or embroidered silk postcards. Strong sunlight will craze lacquer items. These, too, should be displayed in a part of the room where there is no direct sunlight.

How you display your collection will, of course, depend on what you collect and the importance of the collection. It is not unusual for some dedicated collectors to add rooms on to their houses just for the display and proper storage of their collections. The late Charles B. Gardner, who amassed one of the most important collections of antique American glass bottles, housed that collection in a glass-walled room built especially for that purpose. The bottles were shown off in glass-enclosed cabinets that covered three walls. Two collectors of carnival glass have built a house in a midwestern state with specially designed, lighted, recessed shelves that highlight their iridescent collection. Rather than spreading a collection throughout the house, many dedicated collectors realize that what they own appears more important when the collections can be seen as a unit. Depression glass collectors search for oak cabinets with curved glass fronts, made during the same time as their glass.

Collectors of small boxes will display groups of similar boxes together on tables where they can be admired as collections. Display your collectibles so that they are easily cared for, add interest to your room, and do not appear to clutter. When grouped together, most collector's items—such as figurines, dolls, old toys, games, photographica, or any of the other categories discussed in this book—will be more noticeable and important.

PART II
COLLECTIBLES, A TO Z

ADVERTISING ITEMS

A history of American business can be pieced together from the match safes, calendars, posters, fans, trays, and many other items that make up this highly collectible category. A variety of items that once were given away to promote products and services now are included in collections that are made up only of advertising art. These objects also are searched for as adjunctive material to other specialized collections.

Inexpensive items that could be printed or embossed were early and effective promoters for American business in the days before mass media. Pocket mirrors backed with brightly printed celluloid are prized collectibles, as are tin trays, needle books, buttonhooks, shoehorns, letter openers, bottle openers, wall posters, and hundreds of other items that could be adapted for printing a message. Within this large collecting category, there are specialties that absorb the interest (and incomes) of collectors.

Most of today's prized advertising collectibles were made in the late nineteenth and early twentieth centuries. Since most were not made to last and had no particular intrinsic value when new, the supply is somewhat limited. As interest in this category has heightened, supplies have diminished and prices for the most desirable advertising giveaways have risen sharply. Many of the more colorful advertising items have been reproduced in recent years. These reproductions are also expensive, since it is not expedient to do color printing on metal or other materials used for the original advertising items. The celluloid-backed pocket mirror, made to slip into a purse or pocket, would be almost prohibi-

tive to reproduce today; the extensive artwork and careful printing of railroad calendars or enameled tin match safes now cost too much to duplicate.

Many of the collectible advertising items represent products that, in themselves, were highly profitable to make and market. The soft drink business, for instance, an American phenomenon, can be traced through the giveaway items used to promote it. Although originally touted as beneficial and healthful beverages that could cure a variety of illnesses, drinks such as root beer, sarsaparilla and cola were later promoted as good-tasting beverages that would do no harm. Advertising items for this industry are at a premium, since they are collected by advertising item collectors as well as bottle collectors. Many of the more colorful trays have been reproduced recently as nostalgic reminders of American business history.

While many collectors specialize in the items given away by one company, others purchase all types of giveaways and use them as decoration in country kitchens or for other informal decoration in homes and offices. Items that were made annually for a period of years, such as calendars, are collected in series. The scarce pieces that complete a series tend to become very expensive.

In the category of advertising giveaways, condition is an important consideration. Since most of the collectibles were not made to last, collectors search for items that are in as good condition as possible. Many advertising giveaway collectors have, of necessity, become experts at restoration of the

Store display poster for a soap company is advertising an offer of a free poster to dress and frame.

Children's feeding dishes were promotional items for Uneeda Biscuits and the Ralston Purina Company.

Campbell Kids postcards, issued in 1913, were one of many Campbell Kids advertising items. Others were dolls, children's dishes and silverware, trivets, and potholders.

types of materials that were used. Few old fans, calendars, and other paper items can be found in pristine condition, but once they end up in a collection, they are repaired and restored and highly prized. They are the survivors of an earlier time in the field of advertising and remind us that the business hype is always with us.

BOOKS:

Advertising Art in the Art Deco Style, selected by Theodore Menten. Dover Publications, Inc., 180 Varick Street, New York, New York 10014.

Collectors Guide to Advertising Cards, Jim and Cathy McQuary. L-W Promotions, Box 69, Gas City, Indiana 46933.

The Collectible Classics from Commerce, Roselyn Grossholz. P. O. Box 8091, Erie, Pennsylvania 16506.

This Is Ephemera, Maurice Rickards. Stephen Greene Press, Brattleboro, Vermont 05301.

Cracker Jack coin, part of series of presidents, was a prime advertising giveaway.

Roy Rogers celluloid mug was an advertising giveaway made by F & F Mold and Die Works, Dayton, Ohio.

Promotional ashtray for tire company has a removable miniature tire.

AKRO AGATE

Akro Agate toy cups and saucers were made in a variety of colors in marbleized glass.

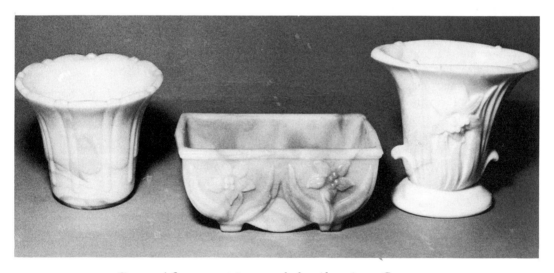

Group of flower containers made by Akro Agate Company.

Although marbles and children's play dishes are discussed in the Toys and Games section, there is a growing specialized cult of collectors of both kinds of items that is more involved with Depression glass collectors than with collectors of other toys and miniatures. They study and search for any glass items made by the Akro Agate Company of Ohio and West Virginia. Glass in unusual marbleized colors and in both clear and opaque bright colors typical of the Art Deco period was produced by this company between the years 1911 and 1952.

The most desirable items for today's Akro Agate collector are the early marbles made before World War I and the children's toy dish sets made between the two world wars. Other production by the company included flowerpots and dishes to place under them, ashtrays, demitasse cups and saucers, and utility bowls. The marbles are difficult to identify today since they are, of course, unmarked. The prime collectible in this category of glass collecting is toy dishes. Marbles found in their original box, marked by the company, are rarities.

Most of the children's toy dishes were packed in sets of six place settings; sets for four were made less frequently. Collectors prefer pristine sets in original boxes, but relatively few of these exist and often collectors put sets together by purchasing one or two pieces at a time. There were a variety of patterns made, but all have a similarity in shape that makes Akro Agate somewhat easy to identify. Handles on cups, teapots, sugar bowls, and creamers are usually unpierced. Surface patterns include panels, raised florals or stippled borders, or interior panels. Along with the tea sets, child-sized water sets were made.

Akro Agate is found in vibrant colors as well as pastel shades, since it was made in both opaque and clear glass. The marbleized glass, for which the company became known, is in great demand by today's Akro collectors. In general, the appeal of Akro Agate has to do with the distinctive styling typical only of the short period during which Art Deco styling was applied to

designs for mass-produced products. The wide spectrum of colors available in the children's dish line and the fact that these colors were "mixed and matched" in the original sets are reasons for their appeal. Within the very broad structure of Depression glass collecting, Akro Agate fanciers prefer to spend their money and time searching for more of the delightful kids' dishes in all the colors and patterns they have memorized.

CLUBS:

Marble Collector's Society
    of America
P. O. Box 222
Trumbull, Connecticut 06611

You will find Akro Agate collectors at Depression glass clubs throughout the country.

BOOKS:

Akro Agate Children's Line, Sophia C. Papapanau. Order from the author, 141 Sedgwick Road, Syracuse, New York 13203.

Collector's Encyclopedia of Akro Agate, Gene Florence. Collector Books, Box 3009, Paducah, Kentucky 42001.

AMERICAN INDIAN ART AND RELICS

Black Pueblo pottery made and signed by Maria and Julian Martinez. Maria, potter of San Ildefonso Pueblo, is considered to be the most outstanding of all twentieth-century Native American potters.

Collecting pottery, fetishes, beadwork, baskets, and other artifacts made and used by Native Americans has, until the last decade, been confined mostly to scholars and museums. It is only within the past ten years that museum displays and publications have drawn the public's interest to this fascinating but long-neglected area of American art and crafts. During this time, also, a renaissance has occurred in the making of fine Southwestern pottery, jewelry, and woven items, and prices for the work of well-known artists have soared. This is partly due to the efforts of some museums in displaying the best of their collections and the resulting excellent publications that have brought attention to the finest artists working in the several media.

Among the most desirable of Native American collectibles are the pots made by Maria Montoya Martinez and her family at San Ildefonso Pueblo in New Mexico, and the work presently being done at neighboring Southwestern Indian pueblo communities. Where once the collector's interest in Indian artifacts was confined to arrowheads dug up in the garden, now there are many collectors of first-rate Indian art and crafts. Although the most important collections are confined to the regions where the art has been and is still being produced, there are people across the country who have discovered that the talents of the American Indian have been put to use to produce accessories that are perfect for the informal style of decorating that has become popular in recent years. These same collectors have also learned that the handsome black pots, colorful rugs, and carefully woven baskets that once were sold by the side of the road for less than a dollar now bring prices in the hundreds and higher. Age is not as important as identification of the artist who made the item, excellence of technique, condition, and intrinsic beauty.

Living Native American artists have frequent exhibits in museums and galleries and there is much work of high quality from which the collector may choose. Older work must be purchased from previous collections and the neophyte collector should read all available literature on the subject and visit as many museum collections as possible before major purchases are made. It is necessary to understand the techniques used by the various tribes in weaving, potting, or jewelry making in order to be able to identify objects, motifs, and materials used. Learn to tell shoddy workmanship from fine craftsmanship. Learn the names of the recognized artists in each field and buy only what is considered the best.

You must also understand something of the history of the various tribes and Native American communities in order to identify regional characteristics in the art forms. If you want to specialize in the work of a single artist, it is helpful to know when and where that artist or craftsperson worked and the methods he or she used or uses in his or her form of art.

Another important aspect for study is the meaning of the motifs used as decoration, whether on rugs, pottery, beadwork, or baskets. Certain contemporary artists have de-

veloped individual styles from traditional motifs and methods and collectors have already learned that investment in this type of updated Native American art is sound. Knowledgeable collectors look for objects that are not the usual tourist souvenir pieces, but genuine works of art done with skill and some originality of design. Modern adaptations of old techniques are often especially beautiful. Of special interest to pottery collectors are the pieces of miniature pottery designed and made by Joseph Lonewolf of Santa Clara Pueblo in New Mexico.

Redware pot, signed by Lela, a Santa Clara potter, has fine decoration and high polish.

White, thin-walled pot, from Acoma Pueblo.

Northwestern Indian carved and painted cradleboard, a fine example of Indian craftsmanship.

This carved pottery is a major investment, but is a safe one. All signed pottery by Maria and Julian Martinez is important as an investment, as are the pots made by Maria and her son, Popovi Da, and Maria's grandson, Tony Da. There are a score of other pueblo potters whose work is innovative and highly prized.

Apache baskets are another form of craft that was carried to the point of fine art. Some of these older baskets have recently risen in value to a thousand times their initial cost. Collectors must learn the types of baskets made by the different tribes in all of the areas of the country. Some tribes still do weaving, but this art form will not go on forever and investing in old or new Native American basketry is a safe way to collect.

Navajo rugs, as investments, also require a lot of knowledge. Many of the contemporary weavers are better at their craft than some of their forebears. Collectors should visit museums and traders to discern the qualities that go into a successful rug or tapestry. There are still a few weavers who are capable of creating rugs that are works of art. Now that the recognized Native American artists are able to demand high prices for their work, more care and talent are put into their creations. It is up to the buyer, however, to purchase with great care in order to realize an increase in value over a period of time.

As techniques in Native American art have improved, information on what is available has increased, also. Read and learn before you invest.

PERIODICALS:

American Indian Art Magazine
7045 Third Avenue
Scottsdale, Arizona 85251

The Indian Trader
Yuma, Arizona 85364

BOOKS:

Hopi Kachinas: The Complete Guide to Collecting Kachina Dolls, Barton Wright. Northland Press, Box N, Flagstaff, Arizona 86001.

Indian Jewelry, Fact and Fantasy, Marsha Lund. Paladin Press, Box 1307, Boulder, Colorado 80302.

The Living Tradition of Maria Martinez. Kodansha International, 10 East 53rd Street, New York, New York 10022.

Modern Pueblo Pottery 1880–1960, Francis H. Harlow. Northland Press, Box N, Flagstaff, Arizona 86001.

Santa Clara Pottery Today, Betty LeFree. University of New Mexico Press, Albuquerque, New Mexico 87131.

Southwestern Indian Arts and Crafts, Tom Bahti. KC Publications, Box 1947, 2115 N. Talkington St., Flagstaff, Arizona 86001.

Southwestern Indian Arts and Crafts, Ray Manley. Ray Manley Photography, Inc., 238 South Tucson Blvd., Tucson, Arizona 85716.

ANIMAL
COLLECTIBLES

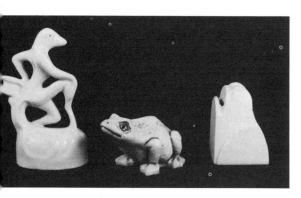

Specialized animal collections can represent all art styles. Left to right: Art Nouveau frog in porcelain; realistic form in pottery; Art Deco frog that is a receptacle for used razor blades (a promotional giveaway for Listerine Shaving Cream).

vorite species, while others collect anything depicting their choice of collector's pet. A collection of cats, for instance, might include fine folk carvings or paintings that rate as expensive works of art. It could also include old toys, stuffed cloth playthings, puzzles, or just ceramic or glass cats. It could include postcards designed at the turn of the century by Louis Wain or rare Egyptian sculpture.

The frog collector might own one of the German porcelain orchestras of six or more members of the genus *Bufo* playing various instruments or a handsome porcelain figure of Art Deco design. Frog owners with a real collector's instinct will find frogs by the

There are many collectors who have shelves filled with toads that might turn into handsome princes at the first kiss of a beautiful woman, but their owners prefer them just the way they are. Often, the gift of one or two ceramic frogs will be the start of such a collection, which grows until the owner has acquired hundreds of artists' versions of the web-footed amphibian made in every material imaginable. The same is true of any other single animal form of fact or fiction. Elephants, unicorns, pigs, owls, horses, cats, dogs, and donkeys are, perhaps, the most popular of the animal collectibles in which people specialize, but there are many other animals that have their following. Snails, monkeys, and rhinoceroses also have their champions in the collecting world.

Some animal collectors search only for *bona fide* works of art that depict their fa-

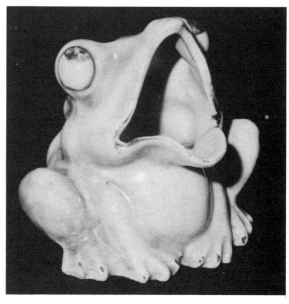

Wide-mouthed frog is a Japanese porcelain ashtray.

Pair of pipe-smoking frogs, made in Japan.

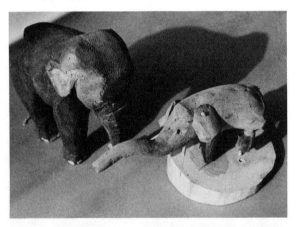

Carved elephants show different perspectives of two well-known folk carvers: (left) circus elephant carved and painted by Bill Brinley; (right) elephant from found root by Dan Ortega.

hundreds jumping off shelves in flea markets, antique shops, and gift stores and the frog lover will eventually end up owning prints, paintings, postcards, needlework, lamps, pillows, and all sorts of items in frog form or depicting frogs. Artists tend to anthropomorphize cats and frogs more than other animals; this is one characteristic that makes these two collecting categories so appealing.

Animal collecting is fun, can cost a little or a lot, and forever solves the gift-giving problem for your relatives. It should be emphasized, however, that a collection is usually worth more than the sum of its parts and as long as there are other collectors of the same animal, your collection grows in value. Many young collectors upgrade their special collections from inexpensive novelty items to fine art as they grow more affluent. If you collect one of the more popular animal forms, you can be assured that there is always someone else who wants them.

BOOKS:

American Glass Animals A to Z
Evelyn Zemel
A to Z Productions
230 NW 126th Street
North Miami, Florida 33168

ART NOUVEAU

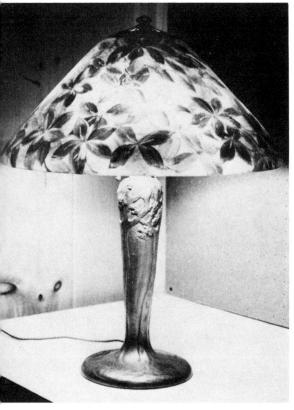

Art Nouveau lamps, such as this Handel bronze lamp with painted glass shade, have risen rapidly in price as Tiffany lamps continue to break auction records.

A particular style in home decoration, jewelry, books and posters, ceramics, glassware, and costume design distinguishes these items. They were made shortly before and for a few years following the turn of the century and their distinctive appearance has strong appeal for many collectors. The style became known as Art Nouveau and is easily identified by the use of sinuous line, fine craftsmanship, and the application of exciting color combinations.

Because the style pervaded every area of decoration for the home and person, there are many categories of collectibles in which one may specialize. There are some collectors whose interest goes beyond one material or type of decorative object. These collectors search for any well-designed and -made object that is representative of the style. Anything, from swatches of textiles to expensive pieces of designer furniture, is in high demand, and since the style was not widely popular when new there is not a great amount from which collectors may choose today. One must watch auctions, know the artists who worked in each medium in European countries as well as the United States, and be willing to part with significant sums when the right desk, chair, or other important piece of furniture comes up for auction. One must also be aware of the few attempts there have been to reproduce this unique style of decoration in order to make sure that investments are sound.

Before you invest heavily in examples of Art Nouveau furniture or other objects, you need to have a thorough knowledge of the various motifs used repeatedly as decoration as well as an awareness of the national manifestations of these motifs. Those collectors who can afford it search for examples of furniture, fabrics, rugs, and wallpapers designed by the leading artists of the period. For the less affluent, there are manufactured items, many of which have some handwork in the decoration. Signatures, marks, and company histories are all helpful tools in identifying objects of the Art Nouveau period. Museum collections and books should be studied, and visits to auction galleries can be instructive. It is also necessary to know what types of objects have been reproduced in recent years. While there have been few attempts at copying furniture, the prices brought by the unique lamps made by Tiffany and others around the turn of the century have encouraged reproduction of the smaller decorative accessories. Some of these are honest reproductions while others are out-and-out fakes. Many of the more fragile decorative objects have so much restoration as to render them worth much less than the prices that are currently being asked.

If a collector of Art Nouveau furniture and decorative accessories cannot take the time to learn everything he or she can find out about the style and workmanship, it is advisable to purchase only through a reputable specialist dealer. Although this is an expensive way of building a worthwhile collection, it is cheaper in the long run. The rewards in Art Nouveau collecting can be great. Many pieces that are included in this category are one of a kind, decorative, and useful. Top-quality pieces are handmade and often signed by the artist; one important desk, chair, or table can become the focal point of a room.

BOOKS:

Art Nouveau and Art Deco Lighting, Alastair Duncan. Simon and Schuster, 1230 Avenue of the Americas, New York, New York 10020.

The Collector's Book of Art Nouveau, Marian Klamkin. Dodd, Mead & Company, 79 Madison Avenue, New York, New York 10016.

The Complete Book of Collecting Art Nouveau, John Mebane. Weathervane Books, distributed by Crown Publishers, One Park Avenue, New York, New York 10016.

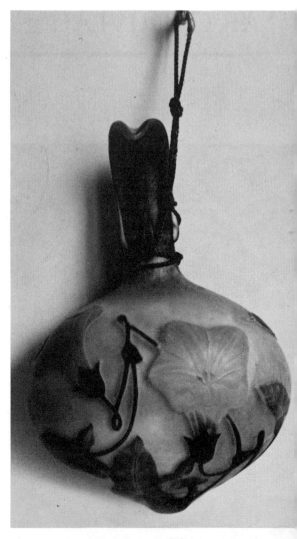

The carved, colored glass of Gallé from the Art Nouveau period has become a prime collector's item.

Louis C. Tiffany's Art Glass, Robert Koch. Crown Publishers, One Park Avenue, New York, New York 10016.

The Painted Lamps of Handel, Joanne C. Grant. The Book Nook, P. O. Box 305, Cornwall on Hudson, New York 12520.

Stained glass window panels, made around the turn of the century, are being purchased as indoor artwork.

BANKS

Metal still banks, once given to children to encourage thrift, are good investments as specialty collectibles.

Children, in the old days, may have started their mornings with a breakfast of oatmeal eaten from an alphabet plate on which was the maxim, "A Penny Saved Is a Penny Earned." The "penny saved" was often put into a wonderful cast-iron bank that made saving fun. You could put the penny on the barrel of a hunter's rifle, pull the lever, and the coin was "shot" into a standing bear. On another bank, you placed the coin in Jonah's hand, pulled the lever, and the coin disappeared into the whale's stomach. There were a great many variations of mechanical banks made, and collectors have been saving them for years. The banks, made in the late nineteenth century, once

sold for less than a dollar; the rarest now bring prices in four figures.

While prices for the old, cast-iron mechanical banks are now so high that they are beyond the reach of the average collector, there are now collectors searching for the later, battery-operated mechanical banks. These were also made as children's toys, were brightly painted, and have complicated mechanisms. Although not as old, if these are found in good condition, they are destined to grow in value.

Collectors of still banks, banks that are usually made in the configuration of animals, buildings, people, vehicles, furniture, or some other shape, have a larger variety

Wooden still bank representing a bank building.

Many still banks were souvenirs of events such as world's fairs or expositions. Some are replicas of real bank buildings; often these were given to children when they opened their first account. Others are souvenirs of places and have the name of the city or tourist attraction where they were purchased.

Still banks are made of a variety of materials, including cast iron, wood, pottery, and glass. Cash registers were a popular configuration as were trunks, safes, and mailboxes.

All old children's banks have some value, but new collectors should be warned that there are many reproductions of both types of banks and a thorough knowledge of this collecting area is necessary before one makes the first purchase.

from which to choose and a smaller investment in each purchase. While prices for old still banks are high in proportion to their original price, a collector can amass a rather large group of interesting still banks without breaking his or her own bank.

BOOKS:

Illustrated Mechanical Bank Book, F. H. Griffith. Order from author, P. O. Box 323, Sea Girt, New Jersey 08750.

Penny Banks: A History and Handbook, Carole G. Rogers. E. P. Dutton, 2 Park Avenue, New York, New York 10016.

BARBERSHOP COLLECTIBLES

Personalized shaving mugs, such as this one, are collected, as are old straight razors and early safety razors.

Now they're unisex and clinical and almost every tool used in them plugs in, but barbershops once were the town gathering place for men to whom their barber was confidant, a source of news and local gossip, and caretaker of a number of sartorial operations from the neck up. Fittings and equipment of old-time barbershops are nostalgic objects for many collectors, some of whom had parents or grandparents who were barbers, and others who simply like these masculine objects.

There are many specialists within the broad category of barberiana. Many collec-

tors specialize in barber's bottles—hair tonic dispensers that were made by almost every glassmaker in the last half of the nineteenth century. These were not commercial bottles, but colorful, long-necked bottles that were filled with the barber's own formula mixed to make hair thick, luxurious, and pleasantly scented. Barber bottles can be found in every type of colorful and clear glass, decorated in all the art glass styles prevalent in the last century.

Another specialty within barberiana is the collecting of shaving mugs. These were personalized with the name of the owner and often were decorated with a scene depicting the client's occupation. Other mugs were decorated with reproductions of famous paintings, patriotic motifs, or symbols of the client's fraternal organization. Most of the shaving mugs found today were made between the years 1870 and 1920. They became obsolete when the safety razor was invented in 1903 and were gradually phased out as men began to shave themselves. Porcelain and metal shaving basins from the same era are also collected.

Straight razors and early safety razors are considered good collector's items. The old straight razors with bone or ivory handles are often displayed in framed cases in well-arranged groupings. The old strops on which they were sharpened are artifacts now, too.

Collectors look for old barber's chairs, shop signs, and early advertisements. Atomizers and old scissors, shaving brushes, and other tools of the barber's trade are part of this collecting scene. Perhaps the most wanted of all items is the trade sign of the American barber, the red-white-and-blue striped pole. If it lights up and revolves, it's a winner.

Barbers filled bottles from their own mixtures of lotions.

Barber bottles in this general shape were made in many colors, with or without decoration.

BEATRIX POTTER COLLECTIBLES

Peter Rabbit and other Beatrix Potter animals decorate this children's dish made by Wedgwood.

First editions of Beatrix Potter books have been prime collector's items for many years. Collectors search for English first editions as well as foreign translations in Dutch, French, Japanese, and other languages; puzzles and toys with Potter characters, panorama fold-out books that were published in limited editions and were especially fragile; children's plates and mugs with Potter characters and quotations from *Peter Rabbit;* and toys made in the forms of the anthropomorphic Potter characters.

Beatrix Potter collectors want anything connected with the author as well as the books she wrote. Any Potter letters that

Money box made by Wedgwood tells story of Peter Rabbit's capture.

Following Beatrix Potter's self-publication of *The Tale of Peter Rabbit* in 1901, generations of children in the English-speaking world have loved the rabbit character and its author. Besides the book and the other twenty-three Peter Rabbit tales written by Beatrix Potter, there are a great many collectibles connected to the children's stories: foreign editions of those books, the many other books written and illustrated by Beatrix Potter (1866–1943), and the toys and figurines made in the likeness of the Potter animal characters.

Flopsy, Mopsy, Cottontail, and Mr. and Mrs. Peter Rabbit toys were offered several years ago as part of the Beatrix Potter Collection.™ They were made by the Eden Toy Company for the seventy-fifth anniversary of the publication of the Peter Rabbit tales.

come up for sale, especially those with illustrations by the writer, are in demand. Peter Rabbit, himself, was first conceived in a letter to a sick friend. Original drawings by the writer of the wonderful children's tales are prime collectibles, also.

Frederick Warne & Co. of London was Miss Potter's publisher in her own country and David McKay published several of her books in the United States. Wedgwood has issued two editions of children's feeding sets with Peter Rabbit motifs and the most recent designs were also used to decorate a money box made by Wedgwood. Warne did not copyright the first edition of *The Tale of Peter Rabbit* and the book was widely reprinted all over the world. The characters have been used frequently by toy manufacturers. Puzzles, cutouts, and coloring books have also been issued from time to time.

Although this category of collecting is sometimes incorporated into larger collections of first editions of children's books, or toys, or children's feeding dishes, there are a growing number of collectors who specialize only in the works of Beatrix Potter and the many objects that her tales have inspired.

BEER CANS AND BREWERIANA

Yesterday's throwaways are often today's collectibles. This is nowhere more apparent than in considering the thousands of people who, within the past decade, have found beer can collecting to be a fascinating and rewarding hobby. It's also a collecting hobby where numbers count: many of the top collectors have amassed huge collections, often numbering more than a thousand cans, within a relatively short time.

Beer cans first appeared on the market in 1935 and are, for the purposes of collecting, divided into two types, the cone top and the flat top. Collectors are aware of each change in material used, types of closures, and regulations governing the beer trade. Cans from all over the world are desirable, and as local breweries have gone out of business or merged with larger companies, only the beer can collectors have become the historians of a fascinating business in which an enormous amount of change occurs within short periods of time.

This collecting hobby is, for many, somewhat uncomplicated and inexpensive. However, those collectors who specialize in cans that represent one region, or one or two companies, and those who branch out into other breweriana such as advertisements, beer trays, calendars, mugs, coasters, or other items, will find themselves investing more in their hobby and also ending up with more valuable and interesting collections.

Old beer cans are found in local dumps and, unfortunately, on roadsides. However, most collectors purchase new cans wherever

Advertising mug for an old Boston brewery.

they travel. Beer cans are further distributed among eager collectors at swap meets or through mail correspondence with other collectors. Condition is an important factor to collectors and, although most collect empties, they want the cans in as near to new condition as possible. On most collectors' wanted lists are cans in unusual sizes,

Groups of collectible beer cans. Collectors search for cans from obsolete breweries, special edition cans, and cans with designs no longer being produced.

foreign cans, cans of unusual beauty, old cans from the 1930s, and all obsolete cans. Cans commemorating special events, whether local or national, are also desirable. Cone tops, which were not made after the early 1950s, are a relatively expensive specialty among beer can collectors.

Beer can collectors take their hobby seriously. They consider it to be a means of preserving the history of a segment of business that has changed enormously in this century. They learn a lot about the packaging of a single product and about the making of that product. They know that bottle collecting started out the same way, with collectors searching dumps and old barns for the relics they were after, and they have watched prices for rarities reach heights never imagined by the earliest bottle collectors. Today's empties can be tomorrow's valued relics.

CLUBS:

Beer Can Collectors of America
P. O. Box 9104
St. Louis, Missouri 63117

The Eastern Coast Breweriana
   Association
Nellie Winterfield, Secretary
961 Clintonville Road
Wallingford, Connecticut 06492

BOOKS:

The Beer Poster Book, Wil Anderson. Cameron House, distributed by The Two Continents Publishing Group, Ltd., 30 East 42nd Street, New York, New York 10017.

Collecting Beer Cans, Richard R. Dolphin. Crown Publishers, One Park Avenue, New York, New York 10016.

The Register of United States Breweries 1876–1976, Donald Bull. Order from author, 21 Frelma Drive, Trumbull, Connecticut 06611.

Universal Beer Can Collectors Guide. Capt. Jack, Inc., 1360 7th Avenue, Marion, Iowa 52302.

BLACK AMERICANA

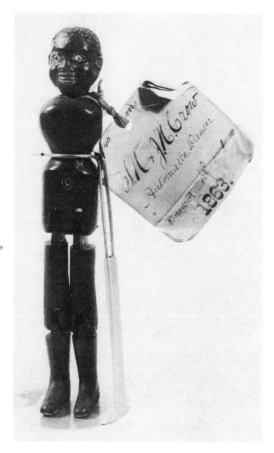

Patent model of "Automatic Dancer" would be one of the prime collectibles in the new specialty of Black Americana.

Currently we are witnessing an explosion in the number of people who are collecting artifacts that have to do with the history of Blacks in American life. For many, this is an attempt to preserve an aspect of our past that will not be repeated, but should be recorded. Formerly, Black collectibles, especially those of a derogatory nature, were collected only as part of other types of collections. For instance, toy or doll collections usually have at least one or two old Black rag dolls, often much worn, but obviously loved. Almost all toy bank collectors would have at least one or two caricature Black banks. Collectors of old sheet music are aware of and own music that dates back to the early part of the last century and depicts Blacks in a derogatory manner. For many, these are "insult" items that are better thrown out than collected. For others, the preservation of this vast store of Black Americana is necessary and desirable if we are to understand ourselves, our past, and our ancestors.

Because the collecting of Black Americana is relatively new, there are still many items to be found. Some are one-of-a-kind handmade toys while others were made in countries that exported novelties and toys to this country in great numbers and pandered to a market that included thousands of Americans who considered these derogatory items to be appealing.

Among the top collectibles in Black Americana are advertising items given away to promote various products. Others are packages that range from tin containers that once held products such as "Mammy's Favorite Brand Coffee" or other foods and beverages. One of the most desirable collectibles in the category of Black Americana is a John Rogers sculpture entitled "The Slave Auction."

Just about anything—including posters,

Frosted glass liquor bottle has a Black man's head as its stopper.

Painted wood carving of a Black man.

Picture postcards from the turn of the century often depicted Black children. These are cards designed by the well-known postcard artist Ellen H. Clapsaddle.

Old sheet music cover is one of hundreds that depicted Black Americans. Most were less complimentary than this one.

books, sheet music, and old phonograph records—relating to Black history in America is desired by collectors; items of a "derogatory" nature are carefully stored as part of America's history. There are many collectors who feel that the unfortunate sentiments of former generations of White Americans can only be instructive if this part of history is not forgotten. This country's treatment of generations of Black Americans can be seen in displays of memorabilia, and perhaps can be understood better through the popular objects that depicted Blacks in a cruel and insulting manner.

BOOKS:

Buried Treasure in the Black Community, Louise J. Gibbons. Vantage Press, Inc., 516 West 34th Street, New York, New York 10001.

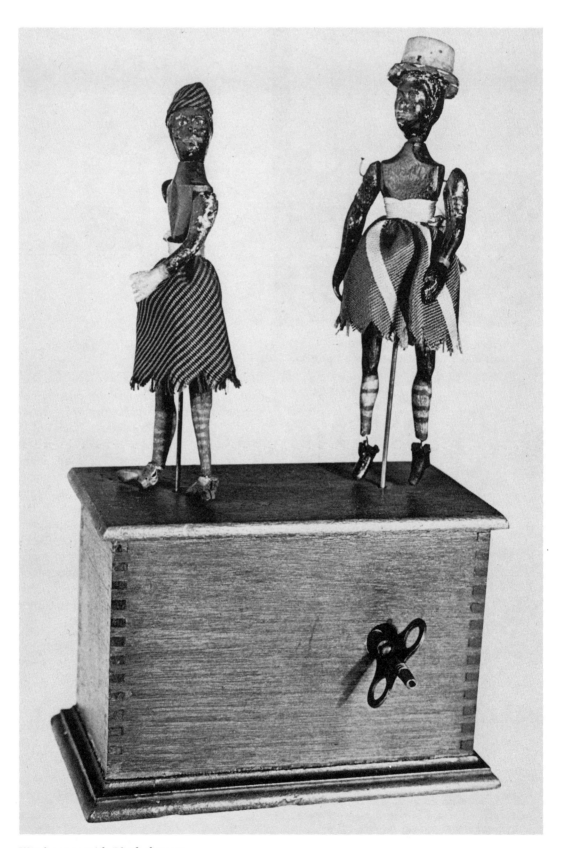

Windup toy with Black dancers.

Licorice penny candy of weeping Black man's face was found in late nineteenth-century apothecary jar in a museum basement.

Black chef was souvenir item of Northern Pacific Railway advertising their slogan, "great big baked potatoe," a dining car specialty.

BOTTLES

Bottle collecting has become one of the most popular and satisfying of all collecting areas, and the subcategories are fascinating. Collections can be put together to suit almost any pocketbook, although it is generally recognized that the most desirable bottles are the eighteenth- and nineteenth-century glass containers made to hold alcoholic beverages. Most of these blown bottles, whether free-blown or blown into handmade molds, are American; they reflect historical events and patriotic personages. Early whiskey flasks are among the first commemorative collectibles, and there are thousands of devotees competing for the relatively few old and perfect examples in rare shapes and colors.

Categories of bottles that are popular among collectors who cannot afford the competitive bidding for old commemorative and historical flasks are ink bottles, scent bottles, old canning jars, milk bottles, bitters bottles, patent medicine bottles, and bottles that once contained such diverse materials as blacking, soda water, beer, soft drinks, and hair tonic. There are thousands of collectors who settle for the hundreds of novelty containers used by the Avon Company to hold their various cosmetics and colognes and others who search for every new figural bottle made to hold Jim Beam Bourbon.

Many collectors of old bottles prospect for additions to their collections by digging in old dumps or abandoned barns and houses. Some attend general household auctions and sales in hopes of finding just one example to add to their collections, while others attend only special bottle auctions where they know beforehand that a unique specimen will be sold. Other collectors limit their acquisitions to bottles that were used locally by long-forgotten businesses. Bottle collectors, as a group, are great amateur historians and pool their information at frequent meetings of clubs formed for that purpose. Frequently, an old bottle found with the remnants of its original label will identify many other similar bottles.

In addition to their interest in the purposes for which certain shapes and sizes of bottles were made, many collectors become

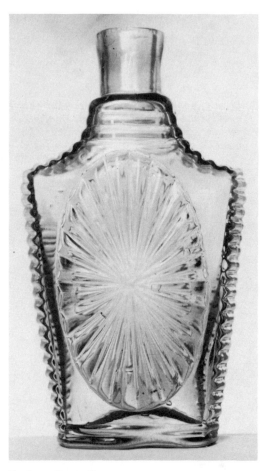

Early and rare Keene, New Hampshire, bottle in pale green glass.

Historical flasks, such as this prime example, are available only to very affluent bottle collectors.

fascinated with the history of the early glass industry and some special collections are formed that contain only the work of one glass house.

For two generations, the bottle collecting world has been very well organized in this country. There are clubs from coast to coast, shows and sales are held frequently, and a lot of private publishing is done to aid new collectors in identification and appreciation of old glass containers. Clubs are open to collectors of any age and bottle collecting interest. Those who are fascinated by old candy containers are as welcome as the people who have collections of historical whiskey flasks. Subjects such as mold marks and closures are discussed and information is published to make all collectors aware of reproductions and fakes.

CLUBS:

Federation of Historical Bottle
    Collectors
Bow Shaw
P. O. Box 106
Penngrove, California 94951

Note: There are local and regional bottle collectors' clubs all over the country. Watch local newspapers for announcements of their shows. Attend a show to get acquainted with the scene and to make contact with members.

PERIODICALS:

Bottle News
Collector's Media, Inc.
Kermit, Texas 79745

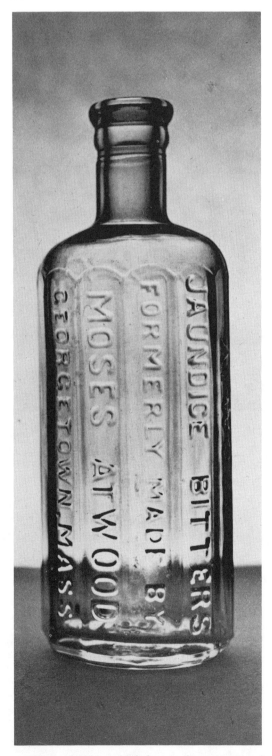

The Glasstique Gaffer
George Kamm, Dept. 608
2479 Lincoln Highway East
Lancaster, Pennsylvania 17602

Old Bottle Magazine
Maverick Publications
Bend, Oregon 97701

BOOKS:

American Glass Bottles, Marian Klamkin with Charles B. Gardner. Wallace-Homestead Book Company, 1912 Grand Avenue, Des Moines, Iowa 50305.

The Collector's Book of Bottles, Marian Klamkin. Dodd, Mead & Company, 79 Madison Avenue, New York, New York 10016.

The Illustrated Guide to Collecting Bottles, Cecil Munsey. Hawthorn/Dutton, 2 Park Avenue, New York, New York 10016.

Bitters bottles, which have a large group of devotees, are an important specialty among bottle collectors.

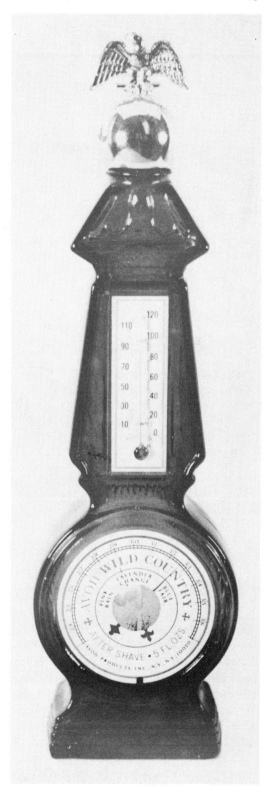

Opposite, above, and right, collectors of Avon figural bottles are active in buying and trading and have their own books and clubs.

BOXES

Lithographed tin boxes, gift packages for cookies or cakes, form colorful and relatively inexpensive collections.

There are specialties within specialties in box collecting. Some people limit their purchases to snuffboxes or other small boxes made for a variety of purposes. Others look for sewing compendia, biscuit tins, tobacco boxes, tea caddies, or Art Deco cigarette boxes. Some collectors specialize in boxes made for a single purpose. Others collect all boxes made in a particular material, such as lacquer, no matter what the original purpose of the box. Still other box collectors purchase all styles, types, and periods of boxes for decorative use in all rooms of a home.

Boxes, in one form or another, have been with us since the start of civilization and have been made of every possible material from solid gold and gemstones to mashed paper or plastic. They may be as simple as the well-known oval Shaker boxes or as complicated as enameled gold Fabergé boxes. The choices for this type of collect-

Box collecting is often confined to a single type or material: small collection of repoussé silver boxes of the last century.

ing are almost endless and there are boxes available to the collector to suit every possible decorative need at prices ranging from a few dollars to astronomical amounts.

Because of the wide range of choices, there are no general box-collecting clubs or societies and few authors have had the stamina to write books on a subject that can be almost endless and would encompass all of the decorative art periods and all of the materials and styles used in the arts. It is seldom that a collector will amass a huge collection of just one type of box. More often, a group of ten or fifteen small boxes will be collected for display together and the collector will go on to another type of box for display elsewhere. While a grouping

of eighteenth- and nineteenth-century tea caddies becomes an interesting and handsome decorative display in a room, most collectors know that the time to stop buying is when the shelves are filled. There are always other categories of boxes to go on to. Music boxes appear to be an exception; the people who collect those are limited only by the amount they can afford to spend. Many of these collectors are mechanically apt and spend their spare time making these old music boxes work.

Since the variety in boxes is almost endless, obviously care and repair of collections would depend on the type of boxes one collects. A fine marquetry box should be repaired, cleaned, and polished by some-

Old store boxes such as this wood spice container are nostalgic collectibles for kitchen decoration.

one who understands restoration of wood, and only a jeweler who is experienced in such things should be called upon to repair a box made of precious metal. Lacquer requires little attention, but cannot really be fully restored if it has suffered damage in the past.

This is a huge category of collecting. However, those who love old boxes will buy whatever they can afford, from steamer trunks to miniature Wedgwood pomade boxes.

BOOKS:

The Collector's Book of Boxes, Marian Klamkin. Dodd, Mead & Company, 79 Madison Avenue, New York, New York 10016.

This French box, containing perfume bottles, is made of ebony with brass inlay.

BUTTONS

For the collector of those small disks that have held every article of clothing together since the time of the Crusades, there is nothing more exhilarating than finding a box of someone's buttons, saved from old clothing over a period of years. There is always the possibility of finding a rare treasure among the ordinary pieces; sorting the savings of parsimonious Victorians often turns up buttons of unusual material or design.

The diversity available in this category of collecting is enormous. Materials used to make buttons over the past centuries include everything from pearl shell to solid gold set with diamonds. Shapes, too, vary from tiny round dots to large and elaborate replicas of flora and fauna. All sorts of art styles can be represented in a comprehensive button collection: there are eighteenth-century hand-painted portrait buttons, Wedgwood jasperware and basalt buttons, buttons in sweeping Art Nouveau designs, and buttons made of old and sometimes valuable coins. The variety is endless, and while some button collectors specialize in one type or material or period, others proudly display all of the buttons they have come by that they feel are worthy of admiration.

One specialization of button is those made of glass, the older ones representing the skills of the glassblower in producing miniature paperweight designs. Iridescent carnival glass buttons were popular at the turn of the century and some were used as hatpins as well as dress ornaments. Every known glass color has been used for button-making; the buttons range from the old, handmade ones to those pressed by machine.

This is a collecting hobby that just doesn't quit. Collectors display their buttons by sewing them to cards in artistic arrangements dictated by type, color, material, or age.

CLUBS:

National Button Society
P. O. Box 39
Eastwood, Kentucky 40018

This organization will put you in touch with a local or regional button collectors' club.

PERIODICALS:

Just Buttons
Sally C. Luscomb
45 Berlin Avenue
Southington, Connecticut 06489

National Button Bulletin
National Button Society
P. O. Box 39
Eastwood, Kentucky 40018

BOOKS:

Button Parade, Dorothy Fisher Brown. Wallace-Homestead Book Company, 1912 Grand Avenue, Des Moines, Iowa 50305.

Buttons, A Collector's Guide, Victor Houart. Charles Scribner's Sons, 597 Fifth Avenue, New York, New York 10017.

The Colorful World of Buttons, Viviane Beck Ertell. The Pyne Press, 291 Witherspoon Street, Princeton, New Jersey 08540.

The Collector's Encyclopedia of Buttons, Sally C. Luscomb. Bonanza Books, Crown Publishers, One Park Avenue, New York, New York 10016.

Button collecting is an old, established hobby with a lot of followers. From a museum display of uniform buttons made in Waterbury, Connecticut.

This New York Yacht Club brass button is a highly desirable item.

Bone and metal button of helmsman at the wheel.

CALENDARS, CALENDAR PLATES, AND TILES

This calendar tile, made by Wedgwood for its Boston importer, is a desirable item for calendar collectors.

There are collectors of old advertising calendars issued in huge quantities in the past. Less abundant and more desirable are the calendar plates made from about 1909 in this country and about two decades earlier in England. American collectors search for plates dating through this century and given away as premiums or gifts to favored customers. Some were souvenir items sold at tourist attractions.

Calendar plates were made mostly of pottery or porcelain, but a few were made of

Reverse of calendar tile shown on page 71.

Calendars advertising railroads appeal to two categories of collectors.

tin or glass. Decoration on the earthenware plates is printed, with the calendar placed by months in the borders or in the center of the plates. The plates were meant to be hung in the kitchen as a wall plaque and many have holes drilled in the back rim.

Many of the plates found today were made by American pottery companies, but some were imports that were either printed to order in Europe or Japan or decorated in this country on imported blanks. A few have some hand-painting, but more often, the name of the advertiser was stamped on the stock annual plate over the glaze and has worn off.

Calendar plates were a better advertising idea than printed calendars. It is easier to throw away obsolete printed material than it is to dispose of an attractive plate that has decorated your kitchen for a year.

Tiles featuring yearly calendars were also made. The most desirable of these for collectors are those made by Wedgwood and used by its Boston importer as annual advertising gifts. The tiles have printed scenes of historical views and buildings around the Boston area on one side and the yearly calendar on the other. These small oblong creamware tiles were made to be collected and there are many collectors who search for them.

Calendar plate collecting is a relatively inexpensive hobby that will yield interesting and attractive display pieces for wall groupings. Along the way, collectors learn a lot about the advertising history of this country and something about porcelain and pottery manufacture and decoration in the first half of this century.

CAMBRIDGE GLASS

Cambridge Glass Company's nude compote in emerald green glass.

Some glass collectors prefer to gather glass of a certain type or period, no matter who manufactured it, while others declare allegiance to the work of only one manufacturer. When patterns typical of the maker are recorded and easy to identify, so that the patterns and colors used can be spotted on a dealer's table, or when most of that company's output is marked, the collectible glass becomes popular. If the glass was made within a limited number of years, is no longer being made, is good quality, and represents the decorative art styles of the years of its production, it is then a natural for collectors. All of the above criteria are what make Cambridge glass so desirable today.

The decorative and useful colored and clear glass produced by the Cambridge Glass Company of Cambridge, Ohio, between the years 1902 and 1954 was hand-made and of exceptional quality. The techniques used in decorating were etching, cutting, enameling, and gold overlay on more than forty colors of molded glass. There is a huge variety of molded patterns and shapes from which to choose, and art styles range from pressed glass in imitation of the cut glass so popular at the beginning of the century, through Art Nouveau and Art Deco,

Cambridge nudes in Crown Tuscan glass. This technique of using a clear glass over translucent colored glass was common in Cambridge glass of the 1920s and 1930s.

Cambridge Glass Company's "Doric" candlesticks with ram's head decoration.

to the unadorned, simple styles of the 1940s. Collectors search for anything made by Cambridge, but an especially desirable collectible is the molded glass swan made in sizes ranging from tiny salt or mint dishes to large centerpieces. These were made in a great range of colors and there are collectors who specialize only in Cambridge swans.

Most Cambridge pieces were marked with a C inside a triangle; a marked piece is always worth more than an identical unmarked piece.

Cambridge glass was quality giftware with well-designed and -executed patterns. Opaque and clear glass can be found. Surface treatment sometimes included iridizing, or partial or complete frosting. The 1903 catalog of the Cambridge Glass Company shows that a huge variety of shapes were made, including water bottles, cruets, covered and footed bowls, covered butter dishes, candy jars, spice sets, stand lamps, a great variety of tumblers and stemware, fishbowls, aquariums, birdbaths, decanters, photographers' supplies, paperweights, food

jars, and jelly tumblers. Novelties included opal baskets and hats, slippers, pen trays, and soap dishes. Glass lamp chimneys constituted a large part of Cambridge's business in those early days.

Specializing in Cambridge glass, with a huge variety of objects made through the company's long period of production, can be a fertile and profitable hobby for lovers of American glassware. The collecting field is an offshoot of well-organized Depression glass collecting, but has its own clubs and good source material for the beginner and the advanced collector.

CLUBS:

National Cambridge Collectors,
  Inc., Dept. D
P. O. Box 416
Cambridge, Ohio 43725

Other clubs where Cambridge collectors can be found are the numerous Depression glass clubs throughout the country. See Depression glass.

Console set made by Cambridge. Base pattern is "Stratford," but dolphin shape was derived from early Sandwich glass design. Color of glass is apple green. The unusual bowl appears in no Cambridge pattern book.

PERIODICALS:

Cambridge Crystal Ball
National Cambridge Collectors,
 Inc., Dept. D
P. O. Box 416
Cambridge, Ohio 43725

BOOKS:

The Cambridge Glass Book, Harold and Judy Bennett.

1903 Reprint of Catalog of the Cambridge Glass Company, Harold and Judy Bennett.

Cambridge, Ohio, Glass in Color—Book Two, Mary, Lyle, and Lynn Welker.

The Cambridge Glass Company, Books One and Two, Mary, Lyle, and Lynn Welker.

The Cambridge Glass Company Catalog Reprint 1930–1934. National Cambridge Collectors, Inc., P. O. Box 416, Cambridge, Ohio 43725.

Note: All of the books listed can be ordered from the above address or through specialist book dealers. See Appendix.

CARNIVAL GLASS

Of all the nostalgic collectibles searched for today, the iridescent, colorful glass made at the turn of the century is undoubtedly the most popular. The value of this once inexpensive glassware has risen in recent years to heights unimagined by those who do not know its history or who are unaware of the fascinating variety in colors and shapes that were made.

The almost endless number of patterns, coupled with the graceful shapes and ever-changing colors, have made it necessary for anyone beginning in this collecting hobby to study it carefully before investing. A further complication for the neophyte collector is that certain shapes and colors have been reproduced in recent years. However, the veteran collector is aware of the reproductions that have been made and there have been publications that warn of new carnival glass production.

As with any collecting hobby that requires more than a casual investment, it is important to know what you are purchasing and to be aware of all the pitfalls of rushing in to invest without being armed with the information necessary to make sound purchases. Carnival glass is no longer "the poor man's Tiffany." It is now a hobby that requires a hefty investment in order to put together a worthwhile collection.

Those who limit their collections of carnival glass to a single shape, such as candy dishes or tumblers, will find the supply has dwindled in the past few years. An all-carnival-glass auction will bring out the many serious collectors who wish to round out their collections by purchasing the one or two available tumblers in a pattern that matches their water pitcher or the sugar

Carnival glass lamp, Northwood's "Grape and Cable" pattern.

bowl that will complete a table set in a certain color and pattern. Some collectors wait for the opportunity to purchase a piece of glass made by a specific company that may have been in existence for only a few years.

Souvenir item of Elk's convention in 1911 is a rarity in carnival glass.

Carnival town pump is a popular item for specialist glass collectors.

The dedicated collector knows which patterns were made by each of the four major companies that produced the glass, what colors these patterns were made in, and how plentiful each pattern is. The colors include the base glass and the surface iridescence and it is the combination of these factors that dictate the ultimate appearance of the glass.

The basic attraction of carnival glass is that it is an American product and the style is representative of a period in the decorative arts that still has strong aesthetic appeal for many. There are enough pieces that were made as advertising giveaways or commemoratives to satisfy the business history buff.

For those who feel more secure in an area of collecting and investment when there are clubs to join and information on the collectible to keep them aware of all facets of their chosen subject, carnival glass is an appealing specialty.

CLUBS:

American Carnival Glass Association
1555 Blossom Park
Lakewood, Ohio 44107

Heart of America Carnival Glass
   Association
3048 Tamarack Drive
Manhattan, Kansas 66502

International Carnival Glass
   Association
Lee Markley
R.R. 1
Mentone, Indiana 46539

Note: All of these three collectors' clubs issue newsletters.

PERIODICALS:

Carnival Glass News and Views
O. Joe Olson
606 East 60th Street
Kansas City, Missouri 64131

BOOKS:

Carnival Glass, Books 1–10, Marion Hartung. Order from the author, Box 69, Emporia, Kansas 66801.

Water set in carnival glass, with peacock-at-fountain pattern. Water sets and tumblers are desirable shapes for collectors.

The Carnival Glass Collector's Price Guide, Marian Klamkin. Hawthorn/Dutton, 2 Park Avenue, New York, New York 10016.

The Collector's Guide to Carnival Glass, Marian Klamkin. Hawthorn/Dutton, 2 Park Avenue, New York, New York 10016.

Some collectors specialize in Northwood's "Grape and Cable" pattern. It was made in many shapes and colors and is easily identifiable.

The elaborate patterns, highly iridescent finish, and massive size of punch bowls make them important collector's items. The name of this pattern is "Fashion."

CASTOR SETS
AND CASTORS

Castor set of pressed glass and blown-in-mold bottles.

Multi-piece serving sets that include parts made of glass frequently did not survive in great numbers. Condiment sets for table use, made in the last century, are fun to look for and collect. Because most were made during a period when our glass factories were producing glass in a wide variety of colors and handwork was still being used,

castor sets have great appeal to lovers of Victoriana. Frequently, the glass bottles and jars were set into stands of silverplate that represent the ornate styles of the last century.

Collectors look for castor sets with bottles of colored glass. Amethyst, cranberry, cobalt, rubina, and Nailsea-type glass were used. The two types of castors frequently found are stands with three or more bottles and jars, and pickle castors, which include one large, wide-mouth jar on a metal stand

Castor set with six parts, in etched glass and silver.

Silver and crystal condiment set, a presentation piece made in 1864, has nautical design.

Castor set, used in officer's mess of Royal Air Force, is an unusual collector's item.

with matching tongs. The ornate sets can include as many as six bottles on a single stand. Blown-in-mold bottles, pressed glass, and etched or enameled glass can be found in castors.

Because some of the castor sets found today once had some hard use, collectors should be certain that all glass parts match and that stoppers and shaker tops are original and in good condition. Metal stands are frequently worn, but can be resilvered without devaluing the set.

BOOKS:

Collecting Brides' Baskets and Other Table Glass Fancies, John Mebane. Wallace-Homestead Book Company, 1912 Grand Avenue, Des Moines, Iowa 50305.

CELEBRITY COLLECTIBLES

There are instances when someone with the collecting instinct identifies strongly with one or more celebrities of the past or present and looks only for items connected with that person. The celebrity may be a public figure who was important to the collector's childhood, a stage entertainer or recording star, a movie star, a heroic figure, or sometimes a group of people connected by profession or birth. Celebrities who fall into these categories may be as diverse as the Dionne quintuplets and Abraham Lincoln. Whoever they are, the one thing they have in common is that there are people who want all items associated with their lives and accomplishments.

Most often, but not always, the celebrity or celebrities are no longer living. The untimely death of one of them, Elvis Presley, caused a huge surge in what was already an established area of collecting. Collectors who bought every recording made by the rock and roll star when he was alive have added items such as T-shirts, bumper stickers, concert programs, jewelry, and all of the mourning memorabilia associated with the singer's death.

Celebrity collectibles are not always such recent novelty items. There are Charles Lindbergh collectors who look for the memorabilia of the aviator's famous flight across the Atlantic in 1927 and all commemorative items connected with Lindbergh. Collectors of Lincolniana purchase folk carvings as well as mourning material, old newspaper clippings, sheet music, picture postcards, and the hundreds of other items associated with Abraham Lincoln.

The publicity that accompanied the fa-

This ceramic bust of rock star Elvis Presley was made as a memorial after his death.

Autographed publicity photographs of a star of the 1940s are collector's items for people who specialize in big bands or vocalists of the period.

mous multiple birth of the Dionne quintuplets on May 28, 1934, led to worldwide fascination with the survival and growth of the babies and a huge industry of souvenirs and products endorsed by their doctor. Dolls, games, toys, and books were produced and articles printed by the hundreds. Paper dolls, feeding spoons, calendars, and postcards are Dionne collector's items.

Beatlemania—collecting everything associated with the talented and innovative rock group—is only a part of a larger collecting area made up of all material associated with this important pop music era. Other rock stars and groups have their followers and collectors, too.

There are as many collecting areas as there are famous movie stars of the 1930s and early Forties. Sonja Henie, Mae West, W. C. Fields, Charles Chaplin, Judy Garland, and hundreds of other celebrities of the silver screen are subjects of somebody's collection of memorabilia. Musicians of the Big Band era, especially the band leaders and vocalists, are remembered through publicity material, recordings, sheet music, and other souvenirs of the prewar era. Some celebrities become the subject for collec-

tions in their lifetime, while others are appealing as collectors' subjects once they have departed.

Celebrity collections are tangible monuments to people who accomplished in life what many of us only fantasize. The objects connected with famous or infamous persons are always wanted by someone to whom the celebrity whose memorabilia he or she collects becomes more real with each acquisition.

BOOKS:

Movie-Star Portraits of the Forties, edited by Jack Kobal. Dover Publications, Inc., 180 Varick Street, New York, New York 10014.

BOOK CLUB:

Nostalgia Book Club
165 Huguenot Street
New Rochelle, New York 10801

Note: This is a combination book club and celebrity collector's club. Membership includes club bulletin, *Reminiscing Time.*

CHILDREN'S FEEDING DISHES

Child's plate is one example of many Staffordshire printed plates made to teach moral lessons to children at mealtime.

Children's milk jug has colorful nursery rhyme pictures.

In the early days of china collecting there were always some specialists who loved the plates and mugs made and decorated especially for children by the Staffordshire potters in the nineteenth century. Sets of feeding dishes were also made in other countries in pottery, silverplate, silver, and pewter. These are not play dishes, but dishes designed to encourage a child to eat until the design on the plate could be seen. Others were gift items, usually given at birthdays, christenings, and Christmas. Mugs inscribed with legends, such as "A Present for my Nephew," or "A Trifle for Charles," were popular throughout the Victorian era. Some were colorfully decorated with transfer patterns of horses or alphabet letters, the latter making every meal a learning experience.

Children's plates, first made in the latter part of the eighteenth century, were produced in great number by the Staffordshire potters. These had borders of embossed or printed alphabets and center designs of

Baby plate with Sunbonnet boy and girl was advertising giveaway for store in Amenia, New York.

heavy, deep-rimmed plates with colorful nursery rhymes and illustrations or advertising pictures that reveal they were promotional items of food companies. By the time these plates appeared, there were established American potters able to produce the plates, milk jugs, and mugs in quantity. Although a great many of these feeding plates were produced, not a lot survived, and the later ABC plates and plates with decals of nursery rhyme characters are recognized as a collectible with a bright future. Look for plates in good condition on which the transfer designs are still visible. The variety to be found, both in shape and pattern, is large; the graphics are sometimes funny, frequently colorful and attractive. Children in this century were not usually exhorted at each meal to pay attention to Dr. Franklin's rules for an honest, if grim, adulthood, and we're more likely to find wonderful decals of nursery rhymes and characters from children's fables on the more recent plates. Borden's Elsie the Cow and the Campbell Kids were only two of the familiar trademarks used on promotional plates. The Ralston Purina Company issued a feeding bowl for their cereal that delivers the message "Ummm, all gone" on its inside bottom surface.

transfer scenes that usually featured children at work or play. Popular with American parents were plates decorated with maxims written by Benjamin Franklin. "If you would know the value of money try to borrow some" appeared through many an American child's string beans.

The nineteenth-century feeding plates are now considered prime collector's items and many have found their final resting places in museums. Only very affluent collectors specialize in the nineteenth-century Staffordshire plates and mugs. A few still appear on the market today, but usually they are not in good condition and they are very expensive.

Most of the collectible feeding dishes purchased by today's collector are from the first half of this century. These are the

There is variety, business history, but most of all, a lot of amusement in a collection of children's feeding dishes and additions to such a collection do not have to be very old to be desirable. There is an entire generation of children today who do not recognize Howdy Doody at the bottom of a dish, nor do they know that their plastic mug portrays Roy Rogers even though their mothers do. Children's feeding dishes have a way of becoming "collectible" in a very short time.

CHRISTMAS COLLECTIBLES

An old-fashioned Christmas is celebrated in many houses by the ritual of taking out cartons of nostalgic decorations for mantel and tree. These collections of Santa Claus figures, bells, reindeer, crèches, wreaths, miniature nativity scenes, and tree lights with figural bulbs are sometimes a family accumulation, saved and added to from year to year. More often, they are deliberate purchases by collectors who haunt garage sales and flea markets in search of old Christmas decorations once saved by someone else.

There are a lot of advantages in searching for and saving Christmas decorative objects from past decades. The investment increases in value each year as the collection grows. From the display of old Christmas material we learn about the subtle changes in the celebration of the holiday and its symbols. Even a collection of old Christmas cards and postcards shows us how Santa Claus evolved from St. Nicholas in a jeweled miter and satin robes to the chubby, white-bearded man dressed in the familiar red costume trimmed in white fur. We can also see that he has put on weight over the years, since the Santa Claus of the cards made in the first decade of this century was lean and had not yet evolved into a single image. Each artist had his own idea of what the character should be.

Christmas tree lightbulbs representing various characters are prized among today's collectors. These were made from the beginning of this century, but the majority of the bulbs found today were sold during the 1930s and were imported from Japan. German bulbs, expensive when new, were the prototypes of some of the later Japanese bulbs and the earliest shapes were Santa Clauses, animals, snowmen, stars, and flowers. The shapes of the 1930s are more imaginative and include Disney characters, comic strip characters, storybook people and animals, and hundreds of familiar objects that were adaptable to the material of painted blown glass. The bulbs were mass-produced; machine-blown in molds, hand-painted in assembly-line fashion, attached to wired fixtures, boxed, and exported by the millions, mostly to the United States. Glass figural bulbs were unobtainable during World War II and the industry was revived for a short while after the war. However, most of the figural bulbs found today are prewar and increase in value each year.

Collectors of Christmas lights also look for bubble lights of the 1940s and the first General Electric twinkle bulbs of the following decade. The true collector's items are the earlier figural lights imported by the Noma Corporation, whose founders first thought of electric lights for Christmas trees as a way of avoiding tragic fires caused by candle-lit trees.

All early Christmas items are wanted by collectors who search, especially, for those made of materials seldom used today. Celluloid animals and other figures are often well detailed. Papier mâché Santas, dressed in paper clothing, can sometimes be found in almost-new condition. All old Christmas items are fun to collect and grow in value as the collection grows in size.

BOOKS:

The Christmas Tree Book, Phillip V. Snyder. The Viking Press, 625 Madison Avenue, New York, New York 10022.

Carved and painted store figure of Santa Claus is a prime Christmas collectible. This folk carving is old and valuable.

Picture postcards from the end of the last century and the first decade of the 1900s show Santa Claus evolving into the standard figure we recognize today.

Fragile old Christmas decorations such as these metallic-covered glass tree ornaments have special value if they were made in Occupied Japan. These have original paper labels.

*Old Christmas ornaments, all marked "**Made in Occupied Japan**."*

COCA-COLA COLLECTIBLES

When Dr. John S. Pemberton developed and marketed "a syrup beneficial to health" (made from root extracts and sugar) in 1886, it was the start of one of the most successful businesses in history. The pharmacist also began an empire that is recorded in a host of relics now collected by many. Early advertising items, which include calendars, bottle openers, trays, pens, knives, and other novelties and soda fountain items, are collected today.

Bottle collectors were the first to recognize the importance of the history of soda fountain collectibles and early Coca-Cola bottles, which include fountain syrup bottles as well as the later bottles used by local bottlers once the syrup was mixed with sparkling water and sold for home consumption. All bottle collectors look for the rare examples of the first bottle used by Coca-Cola. It was designed by Alex Samuelson in 1915 and the "hobble skirt" shape rapidly became identified with the drink and helped to popularize the product. All variations on this bottle shape are collected, as well as later cans and packaging used by the company through its long and successful history.

All store items are especially desirable to collectors, who look for dispensers, fountain glasses, posters, advertising signs, and even the large red coolers. Service trays are high on the list of all "Coke" collectors, who search for trays of the 1930s and Forties as well as any earlier ones they can find and afford.

Playing cards, nature study cards issued in 1930, blotters, books, and bottle openers are all desirable items used by the company to attract children and adults to their product. The company also gave away movie star cutout books in the 1930s. Other desirable collectibles are objects made by Coca-Cola during World War II as gifts for servicemen. These include playing cards, Bingo cards, sewing kits, and games. Another type of wartime collectible in this category is cutout display cards of American servicewomen.

Miniature Coca-Cola bottles in glass, as well as the later plastic miniatures, are sought after, and toy delivery trucks are high on every Coke collector's list. All of the small novelty advertising giveaways are collected; these include watch fobs, thermometers, keychains, rulers, book matches, and pencil sharpeners.

A leaded glass Tiffany shade, an in-store promotional item, is probably the top collectible in this field. There are few of them around and they seldom come up for sale. Collectors are aware of the many reproductions that have been made in recent years as nostalgia items and are careful when purchasing this colorful collectible. Almost as desirable as the original Coca-Cola lampshade are pottery soda fountain dispensers and oak syrup barrels.

Coca-Cola bottles representing as large a geographical area as possible make up the bulk of most collections. One of the prime items in this category is a flashed gold commemorative bottle made as a presentation piece to bottlers who celebrated their golden anniversaries with the company. Any item with the familiar registered trademark is desirable; they can be found almost anywhere in the world.

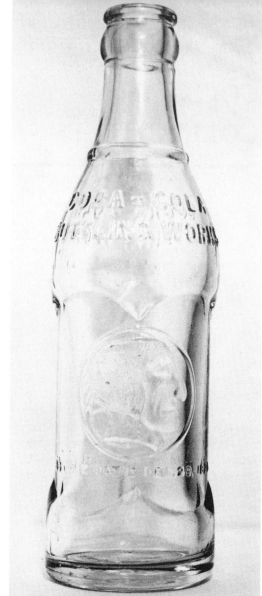

CLUBS:

The Cola Clan
Bob Bullaloe
3965 Pikes Peak
Memphis, Tennessee 38108

Coca-Cola Clan
Box 13479
Arlington, Texas 76013

PERIODICALS:

Coca-Cola Clan Newsletter
Don Smith
Box 13479
Arlington, Texas 76013

BOOKS:

The Coca-Cola Company, An Illustrated Profile. The Coca-Cola Company, Box 1011, Atlanta, Georgia 30301.

The Illustrated Guide to Collectibles of Coca-Cola, Cecil Munsey. Hawthorn/Dutton, 2 Park Avenue, New York, New York 10016.

Official 1977 Price Guide to the Illustrated Guide to the Collectibles of Coca-Cola Et Cetera, Cecil Munsey. Nostalgia Publishing Company, 21 South Lake Drive, Hackensack, New Jersey 07601.

Coca-Cola collectors often branch out to include other advertising items for soft drinks. Hires Root Beer mugs were store items of late 1900s.

Opposite page and above, all glass bottles from Coca-Cola made before plastic bottles or cans are collector's items today.

Hires mug made in Germany by Villeroy and Bosch.

COMIC BOOKS

Those ten-cent color comics that thrilled and entertained children thirty or forty years ago are now popular collector's items that are traded and sold for many times their original cost. Collectors search for first issues and complete runs of the books that depicted superheroes and heroines, cartoon characters, and classic stories in colorful artwork. Superman, Batman, and Wonder Woman all had their birth as comic book characters and only later became television heroes. When they moved from the covers of paper books into TV-land, sales of comic books fell off and the "golden age" of comic book publishing was, for purposes of collecting, proclaimed to have been the years from the late 1930s to 1950.

The comic book evolved from publications called Big Little Books that were popular in the second decade of this century. These were small, hardcover books of comics with a frame to a page. Through these books, a generation was introduced to Tarzan, Flash Gordon, Tailspin Tommy, Roy Rogers, Orphan Annie, and other real or imaginary characters. These were bought for ten cents and read, reread, and traded. Once color comic books were introduced in the late 1930s, Big Little Books were no longer printed.

Comic strips have been published since the end of the last century, and a few were published in book form. However, once the comic book format, colorful and cheap, was devised, thousands were put on the market and, despite warnings from educators that they were harmful for children, found their way into the hands of almost every American child. Today, collectors search for comic books that will fill in holes in almost-completed runs. Original artwork, especially that drawn by the best-known artists of the "golden age," is a most desirable item to comic book collectors.

Comic book collecting is a world of science fiction, crime fighters, rags-to-riches characters, magic and occult, and comedy. *Blondie* by Chic Young, *Li'l Abner* by Al Capp, *Terry and the Pirates* by Milton Caniff, and *Buck Rogers in the Twenty-fifth Century* by Phil Nowlan and Dick Calkins were followed in the daily papers and their stories were then compiled into comic books where a child didn't have to wait for the next installment to find out how the story would end.

Today's comic book collector is interested only in the books, themselves. However, there are offshoots of this collecting era. There are Popeye collectors who want not only the books and artwork, but all the toys and other items made that represent the imaginative and amusing Elzie Segar characters. Games, toys, banks, dolls,

Big Little Books were forerunners of paperbound comic books and are in demand by collectors.

Comic books are nostalgia items wanted by many devoted collectors.

watches, rings, and other items featuring Popeye, Olive Oyl, and Wimpy are in this category. When the cartoon characters jumped off the printed page into radio, there were advertising giveaways offered and Dick Tracy decoder rings, Orphan Annie Ovaltine mugs, and other items are all collected by today's nostalgia buff.

There appears to be more than just nostalgia involved with comic book collecting. The rare items have increased in value to an amount that exceeds by many points the increase in rare book values. This is a relatively recent popular collectible in which early investment has already paid off.

CLUBS:

Comic Art Collectors
Orlando Cox
561 Obispo Avenue
Orlando, Florida 32807

BOOKS:

Classic Comics and Their Creators, Martin Sheridan. Post-Era Books, Box 150, Arcadia, California 91006.

The Comic-Book Book, edited by Don Thompson and Dick Lupoff. Arlington House, 165 Huguenot Street, New Rochelle, New York 10801.

The Comic Book Price Guide, Robert M. Overstreet. Crown Publishers, One Park Avenue, New York, New York 10016.

Comic Strip Toys, Kenny Harman. Wallace-Homestead Book Company, 1912 Grand Avenue, Des Moines, Iowa 50305.

A Guide to Collecting and Selling Comic Books, Raymond Carlson. Pilot Books, 347 Fifth Avenue, New York, New York 10016.

COMMEMORATIVE
CHINA
AND GLASS

Creamware jug commemorating America's first President was made in the Staffordshire region of England.

Wedgwood's commemorative basalt bust of Winston Churchill.

Politics and patriotism are two subjects that have been commemorated on ceramic and glass objects for centuries. Heroes and villains also have their commemorative plates, jugs, mugs, and dishes. Tiles, ashtrays, clay pipes, bowls, and figurines have been made to commemorate people, places, and events. These are all collector's items wanted by someone.

People collect all ceramic items enhanced by depictions of historic houses or other

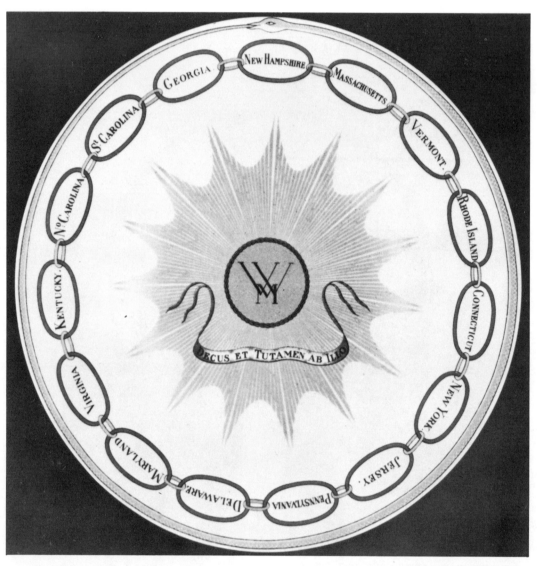

Haviland plate for the American Bicentennial is a reproduction of Martha Washington's china pattern.

buildings. Decorated plates made by Staffordshire potters for the American market have been so successful a segment of their business that they continue to be made to this day. National tragedies and great celebrations have been memorialized on ceramic shapes; some of these plates, cups, vases, or figurines, although they were inexpensive when new, are high-priced and desirable museum pieces today.

Categories within this rather broad field of collecting are blue-and-white printed Staffordshire plates with American patriotic themes, Wedgwood jasperware or basalt medallions or plaques with famous American figures in bas relief, Liverpool jugs that commemorate American ships and their captains, or inexpensive plates commissioned by political campaign committees as giveaways for fund-raising events.

Glass items of a patriotic or political nature were very popular throughout the history of this country. The earliest glass of this type is historical flasks and bottles,

Minton's commemorative vase in Art Deco style, limited edition.

but molded and etched glass in other shapes was also made and is highly collectible today.

Ceramic and glass items of a commemorative design or decoration are lasting reminders of the people, places, and events they were made to represent. Although many were made in huge quantities, some always got broken. Other issues were limited editions and are scarce. Value will depend on what the item is, when it was made and by whom, and the subject matter depicted on it. Often age is not as important as scarcity. For instance, a Wedgwood china tea set in the "Liberty Pattern" was the only china made during World War I to commemorate that event. It was made to raise money for war relief and sold in limited quantities to special and important people in the allied countries. It was never sold in stores and the plates for the design were destroyed when the war ended. This is a prized collectible among knowledgeable commemorative collectors.

There are collectors who specialize only in Wedgwood's commemorative plates made for the American market. Others want only ceramic or glass items that are political campaign items or souvenirs of the Centennial Exposition. This is a large area of collecting with many specialties.

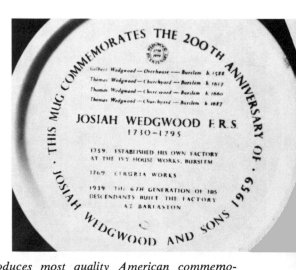

Wedgwood, the British company that produces most quality American commemoratives, occasionally commemorates itself. Creamware mug made in honor of Wedgwood Company's two-hundredth anniversary in 1959.

CORONATION CHINA

Wedgwood teapot in special shade of blue in honor of the coronation of Queen Elizabeth.

You don't have to be an Anglophile to be a collector of china made to commemorate Great Britain's coronations, but there's no question that it helps. There are more collectors of the pottery and porcelain souvenirs made to commemorate the investitures of England's kings and queens than one might think. While most specialize in the commemorative pottery and porcelain turned out for these special events by the great potters of the Staffordshire region, others include all souvenirs of coronations and occasions of national moment in England's history.

Coronation china is produced in some quantity and sold for a limited period after the ceremony has taken place. Great care is given to choice of designer and decorating artist for the pieces that are made, and Britain's potters compete in producing artistic and tasteful pieces. The leading makers in this century have been Spode, Minton,

Jasper plaque made by Wedgwood for the anticipated coronation of Edward VIII, an event that never took place.

Sweetmeat dish commemorates visit of King George VI to United States in 1939.

Coronation mug made for Queen Elizabeth II of England.

Royal Doulton, and Wedgwood. The year 1936 is the outstanding one for coronation collectors, since there were three monarchs in that year and commemorative pottery was made for all. Edward VIII's coronation never took place, but potters were at work designing and producing the expected souvenirs and presentation pieces in anticipation of the event. So many were made that there are collectors who specialize only in Edward VIII china souvenirs. Along with this, they save anything else having to do with the king who abdicated to marry an American.

Coronation souvenirs have been made in quantity since Victoria's investiture in 1837. By this time, Staffordshire potters were well established and were able to produce large amounts of identical items that could be sold cheaply. Victoria's long reign (to 1901) precluded any additional coronation material from the nineteenth century, but other commemorative items are available— enough so that one can collect only ceramics commemorating Victoria and Albert. Most coronation china is, of course, of this century, but there is enough variety in the china made for Victoria's five successors to make up very large collections. There are also, of course, objects made in silver, glass, and other materials that are equally desirable.

Many collectors search for a single shape in coronation china. Mugs are given away to school children to commemorate each coronation. Potters vie with each other for this large-volume business and American dealers buy all they can find second-hand. These are snapped up by specialist collectors of coronation cups. This is a fascinating and not very expensive hobby for the china lover who also is interested in the history of the British royal family. Collectors have coronations, jubilees, and Prince Charles's investiture as Prince of Wales recorded on plates, mugs, money boxes, sweetmeat dishes, plaques, and ashtrays.

CLUBS:

Commemorative Collectors Society
25 Farndale Close (off Wilsthorpe Road)
Long Eaton
North Nottingham, United Kingdom

(Publishes *The Journal of the Commemorative Collectors Society.*)

COUNTRY STORE
COLLECTIBLES

These days, the most valuable item to have collected from an early country store would be the potbellied wood stove around which all the town's Norman Rockwell characters huddled during cold winter days. Unfortunately, too many of these stoves were sold for scrap years ago and most country store items that come up for sale today are the food containers, measures, crocks, bottles, scales, butcher blocks, cutlery sets, cash boxes, and cash registers that were used in general stores well into this century.

All advertising and promotional items made through the nineteenth century and up to World War II are in great demand by collectors across the country, who find fascination in lithographed posters for soap or counter jars for Planter's Peanuts. Old orange crates, especially those still bearing colorful labels depicting the Land of Sunshine, are wanted, although there are many collectors who settle for the labels only.

Commercial food containers printed in the art styles of an earlier time are always in strong demand. These disposable reminders of the past did not survive in great numbers. A collection of them represents the history of packaging at a time when the art of colorful lithography was in its prime. Decal-decorated cracker tins and glass bins are now considered decorative objects for kitchens and informal dining rooms, while old country store items decorate family bars and playrooms.

Millions of Americans travel many miles and pay a lot of money to see reconstructed country villages and stores, which have become popular tourist attractions. The influence of nostalgia for the old days has

Finding old country store boxes with the contents intact is unusual, but box or bottles would be collector's items.

led to the preservation by thousands of collectors of country store items that create lively competitive bidding every time they come up for auction. The fact that so many people desire these decorative and nostalgic items has also led to the reproduction of this type of collectible. As with any other popular, collectible type of object that is

not difficult to reproduce if the demand is there, country store collectors should know what they are buying, what has been reproduced, and what the market is. The best and most obvious source for good and authentic country store items is to follow local auctions and watch for those few auctions of old stores that have recently been closed. If a store has been in business for a long time—even if it has been modernized during its long history—there should be some items that have been kept or that remained in storage for enough years to make them worth adding to a collection.

All old country store items are of interest to someone. Some businesses that started years ago have recently become entranced with their own histories and, although few ever saved their own packages and advertising items when they were new, many now are interested in buying anything that relates to their business history. Many collectors had the foresight to realize the value of some of these items long before the companies that produced them. Items that have special value are those made as promotional advertisements for display in a store. These

These old country store containers are all made of wood.

were limited in number when produced and were discarded as soon as the next attractive display item arrived. A perfect example of this would be promotional display placards for Campbell's soups featuring the two children the company used in its ads. Any early advertising item that is colorful and part of America's advertising history is in demand today.

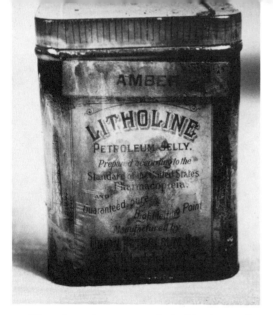

Tin store boxes are desirable items for country store collectors.

Perpetual calendar and bill-filing box with cash drawer is an item from an old country store.

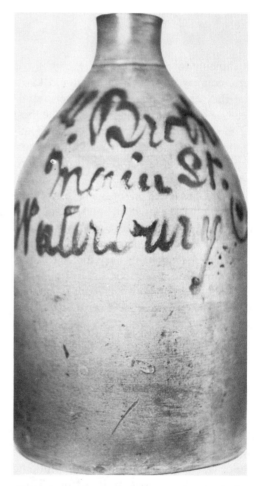

Pottery crocks and jugs are part of the country store collecting scene.

CUT GLASS

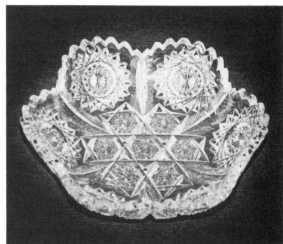

Two cut glass bowls from the brilliant period.

From 1890 and for two decades into this century the art of cutting into thick glass reached a peak of perfection that probably will never be seen again. The hand-cut thick glass cake baskets, decanters, cruets, punch bowls, stemware, and other objects were made in all glass-producing countries of Europe and a collection of them, or often even one or two pieces, gave status to newly settled Americans. It sparkled and dressed up the table as no other glass could. The thirty years of great popularity of this glass is known today as the "brilliant period" of cut glass and there are many new collectors who have respect for the workmanship of the deep cutting and the quality of the glass.

Elaborately cut glass, which requires talent, time, and knowledge, is not made in any quantity today. Some glass is still being produced in Ireland and England and the Waterford Company is notable for its stemware, small gift items, and a few larger works that they produce. The development of glass firms able to turn out huge numbers of items in pressed glass made glasscutting a lost art. Collectors are aware that the brilliant, heavy cut glass that their mothers and grandmothers coveted will probably never be reproduced.

Cut glass of the brilliant period sold at auction only ten or fifteen years ago for a few dollars. No one seemed to want it and it was considered impractical, overly elaborate, and too heavy to be useful. More recently, bidding on any piece of brilliant cut glass is active and prices have begun to soar, especially for the unusual large pieces that are intricately cut and elaborately shaped. Decanters, centerpiece bowls and epergnes, dresser sets, and cruet sets are in great demand.

Cut and engraved glass boat-shaped serving dish. Once ignored by glass collectors, old cut glass is now recognized as the product of a vanishing art.

BOOKS:

American Brilliant Cut Glass, Bill and Louise Boggess. Crown Publishers, One Park Avenue, New York, New York 10016.

American Cut and Engraved Glass, Albert C. Revi. Thomas Nelson, Inc., 405 Seventh Avenue S., Nashville, Tennessee 37203.

American Cut Glass for the Discriminating Collector, Dorothy and Michael J. Pearson. Order from the authors, Box 2844, Miami Beach, Florida 33140.

The Standard Cut Glass Value Guide, Jo Evers. Collector Books, P. O. Box 3008, Paducah, Kentucky 42001.

CLUBS:

The American Cut Glass Association
Connie Harwood
1891 Mt. Vernon Place
Atlanta, Georgia 30338

The National Early American Glass Club
55 Cliff Road
Wellesley Hills, Massachusetts 02181

DEPRESSION GLASS

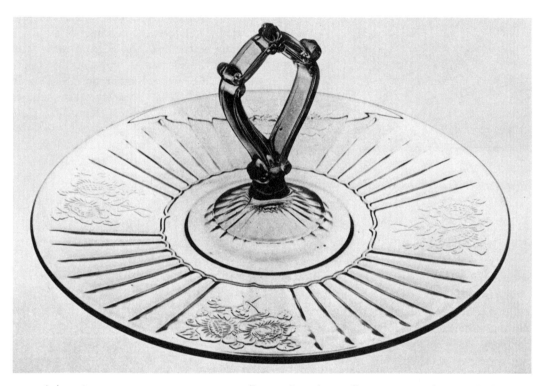

A favorite pattern, now scarce, among Depression glass collectors is Mayfair, made by Federal Glass Company. Cookie jar and cake server are desirable shapes.

During the late 1920s and throughout the following decade the American glass industry survived hard times by manufacturing cheap sets of glass dishes in a variety of colors and molded patterns. Because these dishes were so inexpensive to make, full dinner or luncheon sets could be sold at retail for less than two dollars. Depression glass items are now collected from coast to coast and there are hundreds of clubs and shows dedicated to this single collectible.

Collectors strive to put together table set-tings of various patterns or colors that appeal to them. The glass is studied, traded, discussed, and bought and sold. Dealers who are now known nationally as specialists in Depression glass are kept busy going from one show to another. The glass plates that were once given away during the Depression to entice people to attend a second-rate movie are now in strong demand and are priced accordingly. Everything in this category of popular collectible is sought after and the specialties include

"Miss America" pattern in pink is a hobnail pattern in Depression glass that has become scarce and expensive.

of the Art Deco period and a few collectors search for the pieces that most reflect that style. There are cobalt blue bowls set into stands made of chrome metal and rayed and tiered patterns that remind one of the glory of the 1930s movie palaces. This glass could have been popular at no other time but the Thirties and it has already proved to be a good investment. Often, the interest in the glass of the Depression era leads collectors to look for other collectibles that are related. Therefore, the purchase of a Shirley Temple cereal bowl, once given away with General Mills products, will send the collector off in search of other Shirley Temple collectibles. Radio giveaways are another related area that interests Depression glass collectors. On the whole, however, this category attracts people who really love the colorful glass, and it becomes their all-consuming interest.

citrus fruit reamers, salt and pepper shakers, early refrigerator dishes and oven bakeware, barware, eggnog sets, and baby dishes.

The majority of collectors put together entire services for eight or twelve in appealing patterns and colors. Once one set is complete, they go on to accumulating another or the same pattern in a different color. Many collectors start sets for infant children and it is not unknown for a few dealers or collectors to start accumulating sets for their pets.

In order to amass even one complete Depression glass pattern in table settings it is almost imperative to belong to a club and attend the shows held by the clubs at least once or twice a year. This is where the glass is found in quantity. It's also where the books are sold that provide all the information concerning what was made, in what colors, and by what companies. To the collector, a Depression glass show is a wonderland of sparkle and color and an exercise in nostalgia.

Depression glass is a commercial product

CLUBS:

National:

National Depression Glass Association
Mrs. Vera Redmond
Route 1, Box 216
Westminster, Maryland 21157

Regional:

Note: At last count there were at least seventy clubs throughout the country. Listed below are clubs you can get in touch with to find out where *yours* is.

Arizona
Arizona Depression Glass Club
Virginia Dunnahoo
3238 East Mitchell Drive
Phoenix, Arizona 85018

California
The Depression Heirs
P. O. Box 401
Redlands, California 92373

Humboldt Area Glass Club
3215 Q Street
Eureka, California 95501

Depression glass in color has the "look" of the 1930s. This is an Art Deco pattern called "Tea Room."

Colorado
The Pikes Peak Depression
  Glass Club
Box 4273
Colorado Springs, Colorado 80930

Connecticut
Nutmeg Depression Glass Club
P. O. Box 74
Plainville, Connecticut 06062

Florida
Central Florida Depression Glass Club
Betty L. Smith
1005 West Clemson Drive
Altamont Springs, Florida 32701

Illinois
The 20-30-40 Society
Mrs. James Varmilya
3725 Kemman Avenue
Brookfield, Illinois 60513

Kansas
Liberal Collectors Club
900 Holly Drive
Liberal, Kansas 67901

Louisiana
Collectors of Rainbow Glass
301 Wild Wood Drive
Houma, Louisiana 70360

Maryland
Del-Mar-Va Club
7420 Westlake Terrace
Bethesda, Maryland 20034

Massachusetts
The Yankee Dee Gee-ers
Ann Lyons
123 Burley Street
Danvers, Massachusetts 01923

Michigan
The Great Lakes Depression Glass Club
P. O. Box 53
St. Clair Shores, Michigan 48080

Missouri
Heart of America Glass Collectors
721 Cambridge Drive
Lee's Summit, Missouri 64063

New Jersey
North Jersey DG'ers
Margaret E. Claudy
19 Chestnut Drive
Glen Rock, New Jersey 07452

New York
Hudson Valley Depression Glass Club
Box 294
Walden, New York 12586

Long Island Depression Glass
  Society Ltd.
P. O. Box 119
West Sayville, New York 11796

Ohio
Western Reserve Depression Glass Club
Henry Bennetts
9164 Lynnhaven Road
Parma Heights, Ohio 44130

Lacy patterns, wonderful colors, and interesting shapes appeal to collectors of Depression glassware. This is a kidney-shaped platter and gravy boat in the "Florentine" pattern made by Hazel Atlas.

Oklahoma
Oklahoma Depression Era Club
Joyce Walker
204 West Dale Street
Norman, Oklahoma 73069

Oregon
Oregon Glass Addicts
Betty Jenkinson
8520 South West Davies Road
Beavertown, Oregon 97005

Pennsylvania
The Fly-by-Night Depression
   Glass Club
Donna Yoder
Rte. 2
Watsontown, Pennsylvania 17777

Texas
Permian Basin Depression Glass Club
Patsy Terrell
2205 East 12th Street
Odessa, Texas 79763

PERIODICALS:

Depression Glass Daze
P. O. Box 57
Otisville, Michigan 48463

Glass Review
P. O. Box 2315
Costa Mesa, California 92626

BOOKS:

The Collector's Guide to Depression Glass, Marian Klamkin. Hawthorn/Dutton, 2 Park Avenue, New York, New York 10016.

Colored Glassware of the Depression Era, Hazel Marie Weatherman. Glassbooks, Inc., Route 1, Box 357A, Ozark, Missouri 65721.

The Depression Glass Collector's Price Guide, Marian Klamkin. Hawthorn Books, Inc., 260 Madison Avenue, New York, New York 10016.

DISNEY CHARACTER COLLECTIBLES

Mickey Mouse, born in 1928, cheered a generation of Americans through the Depression and gained another generation of fans who grew up as television viewers of the Mickey Mouse Club. Both generations presently collect Walt Disney's famous cartoon character and licensed objects, made by the thousands, that represent all of the well-known characters developed by the Disney Studios. To children who grew up in the 1930s and Forties, the characters in *Snow White and the Seven Dwarfs, Fantasia, Pinocchio, Bambi, Cinderella,* and *Sleeping Beauty* were real and a memorable part of their childhood. Mickey and Minnie Mouse and Donald and Daisy Duck are two of their favorite movie couples and Ferdinand the Bull and Dumbo the Elephant were childhood friends.

Within the collecting field that has become known as Disneyana there are many specialties. Books, toys, games, watches, clocks, puppets, children's cutlery, dishes, dolls, figurines, toothbrushes and holders, radios, jewelry, and musical instruments are just a few of the items issued in the form of Disney characters or with the characters as decoration. Disney art, especially the celluloids, painted by the thousands for each animated scene, are prime collector's items. Posters and advertisements for the films, as well as advertisements for any of the Disney toys or other objects, are also wanted by collectors.

Toys that have great popular appeal among collectors of Disneyana are those that are animated—usually tin windups.

Old Mickey Mouse children's watches, made by Ingersoll, have escalated in price within the past decade. Mickey Mouse-decorated porcelain toy children's dishes, made in Japan in the 1930s, are valuable today, especially if they can be found in the original boxes.

Within the category of Disney dolls can be found bisque figurines of Snow White and the Seven Dwarfs, but they were also reproduced in hard rubber or composition. Chalk figures of Pinocchio, Goofy, or Pluto can be found, and rubber squeeze toys were made of almost all Disney animal figures.

Among the toys that were made were card games, board games, pull toys, tops, trains, trucks, cars, wagons, cleaning toys, sleds, and musical instruments.

Of the hundreds of children's items made that represented the famous Disney characters, only a small percentage lasted. When these are found by collectors in good to excellent condition, they bring high prices.

The present generation of Disney lovers have new issues of objects made each year to represent the imaginary animals and people who have come out of the Disney Studios. Many of these instant collectibles are made to be sold at the two large Disney amusement parks, while others are licensed products that still have popular appeal. This age of high technology has led to the manufacture of more Disney items for children. Today's Mickey fans can wake up to the sound of the mouse's squeaky voice telling them through their "Mickey Mouse Alarm Clock Choo-Choo" to "Wash your face and

Disney character doll dishes are pieces from two different sets. (Right) Early version of Mickey and Minnie Mouse. Plate with luster border, made in Japan. (Above) Covered tureen with underdish of figures from "Snow White and the Seven Dwarfs."

hands, brush your teeth, and *don't* forget to wind the clock!" What it doesn't tell them is that this is sure to be tomorrow's collector's item.

BOOKS:

Disneyana, Cecil Munsey. Hawthorn/ Dutton, 2 Park Avenue, New York, New York 10016.

Toy dish, made in Japan, with one of Snow White's dwarfs.

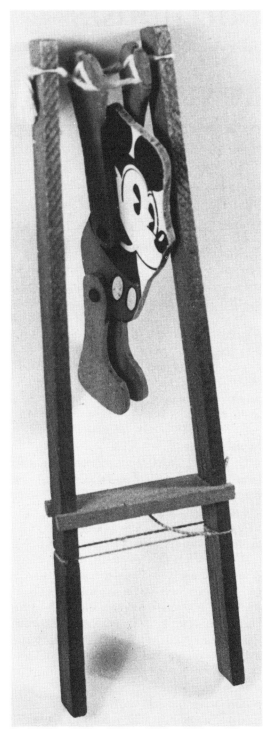

Mickey Mouse squeeze toy, made in early 1940s. When sticks are squeezed, Mickey does acrobatics which vary according to pressure put on the sticks.

DOLLHOUSES AND MINIATURES

Picture yourself as the owner of an authentic Victorian mansion complete with inglenooks and turrets, or a Southwestern adobe hacienda decorated with Navajo rugs and pueblo pottery, or an eighteenth-century townhouse with wing chairs, canopy beds, braided rugs, and brightly lighted brass chandeliers. Thousands of people of modest means *do* own one of these "second homes" and some even have mortgaged their first homes to create or purchase such an extravagant indulgence. The fantasy land of rooms and houses, existing mostly on a scale of one-inch-equals-one-foot, has become one of the fastest-growing collecting hobbies in the United States.

Once a hobby for the very rich, indulging their privileged children, and for a few members of royalty, dollhouses and their furnishings are so appealing that there exist today hundreds of fine craftspeople who specialize in scale-model house-building and furnishings that cover the entire range of architecture and decorative arts made in full size over the past three centuries. These hobbyists now have at their disposal entire hardware stores and lumberyards in miniature from which to select the materials needed to design and make scale-model authentic reproductions of houses and furnishings in almost any style. Ingenious craftspeople have devised methods to manufacture just about anything needed to complete the decorations of a wide variety of styles in dollhouses. Some hobbyists, who started making furnishings or accessories for their own miniature houses, have built their ideas

into big businesses. One retired toolmaker in Connecticut has become enormously successful by supplying brass andirons and electrified candlesticks to dealers and collectors. Other small companies in the miniature world make scale-printed silk fabric for upholstery and wall coverings, and one firm offers thirty-five individually handcrafted chandeliers, hanging fixtures, sconces, lamps, candelabra, and candlesticks complete with Austrian cut crystal and hand-blown glass globes, with metal parts in solid brass finished with 23-karat-gold plating. Some of these can be electrified, and there are kits available for the house wiring.

In the world of miniatures there are now kits available in scale size for just about anything. You can build your own tallcase clock complete with brass pendulum; you can needlepoint your own Aubusson rug; you can embroider an "authentic" chenille coverlet for your "authentic" four-poster. Brass curtain rods are available, as are kits for making period flower arrangements or decorative plants. Hardware supplies are almost endless and you can find wrought-iron HL hinges for your early American kitchen cabinets or polished brass doorknobs and hinges for a more formal setting.

The miniaturist collector is not stuck with just any old house. There are custom builders who will build to your own blueprints or drawings and you can be certain that everything will be "authentic." There is no shortage of dollhouse-scaled brick, roofing shingles, mantels for any style house, flooring, or

Shaker rooms, scaled 1 inch to 1 foot, are authentic in every detail and illustrate the quality of contemporary miniaturists' work.

molding. You can also buy a book that has cutouts for dollhouse stained glass windows (you color them and install them yourself), or another book that gives you sheets of dollhouse floor patterns in tile or brick to be pasted on the floor.

If you do not fantasize living in your doll-house yourself, there are scale-model ready-made families to install as permanent tenants. However, they do not pay rent and it is seldom the initial cost of a dollhouse, but usually the furnishings and upkeep, that make this hobby an expensive one.

As an alternative to building or buying

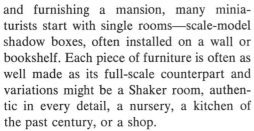

Many of the miniature dishes found today were made in Japan. Tea sets and cocktail sets were made before and after World War II.

and furnishing a mansion, many miniaturists start with single rooms—scale-model shadow boxes, often installed on a wall or bookshelf. Each piece of furniture is often as well made as its full-scale counterpart and variations might be a Shaker room, authentic in every detail, a nursery, a kitchen of the past century, or a shop.

The collecting of miniatures has become one of the fastest-growing hobbies, probably because it includes opportunities for making one's own objects as well as collecting things made by others, both in the past and presently. Furnishing and decorating a single house can become a lifetime job. It requires infinite patience and superb eyesight if the house is to be furnished by the do-it-yourselfer. Perhaps the ultimate in dedication to the one-inch-to-one-foot world

is Mosaic Press, which publishes scale-model original books for dollhouse libraries. This publisher will send out, on request, a set of author's guidelines on *"How To Write a Miniature Book."*

In truth, the mini world is gigantic in terms of collecting and the amount of business it generates among hobbyists. Profits have been big for those capable of thinking small.

Anything for the full-size home can be found today in miniature. Here is a dollhouse-size patio set made in the 1930s.

CLUBS:

Hello Dolly Miniature-of-the-Month Club
Dept. 59
1235 Second Avenue
New York, New York 10021

The National Association of
  Miniature Enthusiasts
1309 Valencia, Suite H
Fullerton, California 92633

PERIODICALS:

Miniature Collector
Acquire Publishing Company
170 Fifth Avenue
New York, New York 10010

The Miniature Magazine
Carstens Publications, Inc.
Fredon-Springdale Road
Fredon Township
P. O. Box 700
Newton, New Jersey 07860

Nutshell News and *Miniatures Catalog*
10 Clifton House
Clifton, Virginia 22024

BOOKS:

All About Doll Houses, Barbara L. Farlie with Charlotte L. Clarke. Bobbs-Merrill Company, Inc., 4 West 58th Street, New York, New York 10019.

Collecting Miniature Antiques, Jean Latham. Charles Scribner's Sons, 597 Fifth Avenue, New York, New York 10017.

The Collector's Guide to Dolls and Dollhouse Miniatures, Marian Maeve O'Brien. Hawthorn/Dutton, 2 Park Avenue, New York, New York 10016.

Victorian Dolls and Their Furnishings, Flora Gill Jacobs. Washington Dolls' House and Toy Museum, 5236 44th Street NW, Washington, D.C. 20015.

Your World in Miniature, Betsey B. Creekmore and Betsey Creekmore. Doubleday & Company, Inc., 245 Park Avenue, New York, New York 10017.

DOLLS

Dollology is a word that rolls off the tongue easily. It means the serious collecting of dolls. There are millions of people of all ages who "own" dolls, but there are thousands of others who collect them. This is a serious hobby and a profitable business for many people throughout the world. Primitive dolls, exquisitely made and dressed dolls, and every possible variation in between are coveted by some doll collectors, while others specialize in dolls made in one country, representative dolls from all countries, dolls made by one maker, fashion dolls from France, dolls of a single century, boy dolls, baby dolls, girl dolls, adult dolls, or dolls made of a single material, such as wax or porcelain.

All races, genders, and ages of people have been reproduced in miniature, and dolls have been dressed to represent almost every occupation. This is an area of collecting that is extremely popular, and the prices for the better-made dolls of the past two centuries have skyrocketed since the hobby became popular in the late 1940s. Peripheral businesses have been in existence since that time and there are local doll hospitals where dolls are restored, repaired, and dressed in reproductions of period costumes. For at least two centuries fine artists have designed and made dolls and that part of the hobby still exists today, with some artists making one-of-a-kind or limited series dolls that are subscribed to before their heads are even out of the kiln.

In high demand are the nineteenth-century German, French, and British dolls produced for privileged children who were allowed to look at, but seldom touch, these expensive toys. A large amount of any doll production *does* get played with and the lifespan of most dolls is so limited that only a few exist of any single model. Even dolls manufactured in great amounts in this century are at a premium. An example of this is the Shirley Temple doll, made in many sizes in the 1930s. Few were put on a shelf out of reach of the recipient. Most were played with and adored and ruined. Those that remain are popular collector's items today.

Today's dollologist can search for the film character dolls such as the aforementioned Shirley Temple dolls, Sonja Henie dolls, the Kewpie dolls designed by Rose O'Neill, Disney character dolls, or the exquisite baby and child dolls designed and made by the German artist Kathe Kruse. There are as many ways to specialize in doll collecting as there are national, occupational, or racial groups of people in the world. This is a hobby that appeals to the child in all of us and there are always new dolls that become instant collector's items. Every people in the world, no matter how primitive, has allowed children to play with some form of doll; in some societies dolls have been awarded special powers of magic and symbolism.

Serious doll collectors are not, as some have said, adults who never grew up. They are usually amateur historians and sociologists who see in their collections the world of people in miniature. They are interested in the history of costume and textiles and do a lot of research to learn the proper accessories and hairstyles of each period.

Their dolls can be almost any size, from tiny miniatures made to live in dollhouses to huge, lifelike babies or children. The dolls of quality that end up in collections are cared for, restored to pristine condition when that is possible, and dressed to appear much as they did when new.

Collections of dolls can be seen at any good quality antiques show, but the best examples are at the doll collectors' shows.

Shakers bought dolls, dressed them in Shaker-made costumes, and sold them at their shops. These are rare and desirable collectibles.

PERIODICALS:

The Doll Reader
Hobby House Press
Riverdale, Maryland 20840

Doll Talk
Kimport Dolls
Box 495
Independence, Missouri 64051

BOOKS:

Book of Collectible Dolls, edited by Kyle D. Husfloen. The Babka Publishing Company, Box 1050, Dubuque, Iowa 52001.

The Doll, Carl Fox. Harry N. Abrams, Inc., 110 East 59th Street, New York, New York 10022.

Dolls, Dolls, Dolls, by Shirley Glubok. Follett Publishing Company, 1010 West Washington Boulevard, Chicago, Illinois 60607.

Eighteenth-century English dolls in original costume.

Doll collectors are beginning to search for Japanese dolls. This boy doll with inset glass eyes, hand-painted features, and hand-sewn robes is a fine example.

EYEWASH CUPS

Eye baths are a collectible that can include glass of many companies, countries, colors, and configurations.

These glass, ceramic, or plastic utilitarian cups were used in the home for attempts at relieving eyestrain, but they are seldom used today, since many doctors believe that their use simply reinfects an already irritated eye. This is a rather esoteric collecting specialty, but one that is growing, since it embraces the work of the glass and ceramics manufacturers of the past two centuries. It has become well enough established as a hobby to inspire the manufacture of several kinds of reproductions in the past couple of years.

Eyewash cups, or eye baths, were made mainly by British and American glass companies and ceramics companies in Great Britain. Those companies known to have made these oval utilitarian cups as early as the eighteenth century are Wedgwood, Leeds, Lowestoft, and Caughly. The finest of these, when they appear on the market, are hand decorated and expensive. Today's collector of modest means searches for examples of nineteenth- and early twentieth-century American and English glass in as many colors and varieties as possible. The McKee Company in Pittsburgh advertised flint glass eye baths in their 1855 catalog and eventually all American makers of utilitarian glass produced eye baths. The small cups, stemmed and unstemmed, were made in clear, amber, green, cobalt blue, milk-white, and red glass, with red being the most scarce. At one time, as recently as one generation ago, everyone had at least one eyewash cup in his or her bathroom cabinet. These collectibles can still be found in garage and house sales or at flea markets for reasonable prices. They vary enough in shape, color, and design to make an interesting display.

FAIRINGS

Seaside and country fair souvenirs became popular in the late nineteenth century in England as German porcelain makers supplied inexpensive small china objects that were sold for small change. These trinkets were brought back from vacation as gifts or remembrances of Margate, Brighton, or other popular resorts in England. Although the bulk of what remains of the objects, now called "fairings," were produced before the turn of the century, they were popular until World War I. Several British potters also produced small figures and figure groups as well as trinket boxes and other porcelain decorations for mantels and dressing tables.

Fairings were made by British and German potters and often were copied by the Japanese. Group on right, entitled "The Welsh Tea Party," is genuine. Group on left is marked "Made in Occupied Japan."

Fairings are distinguished from other porcelain figurines in that they were made to sell cheaply, were made in molds and often hand-painted under or over the glaze, and are usually only three or four inches high. They were mass-produced and decorated in assembly-line fashion. They have a kind of charm for collectors who like popular objects of the past, and their price today as collectibles is high compared to their original cost.

Some fairings were in the form of miniature furniture and are amusing today because they repeat the kind of Victorian clutter that they represent in miniature. One might find a small porcelain dressing table covered in tiny scent bottles, jewelry, and other items. Replicas of other pieces of furniture are often found as well. These were not toys for children, but were one more decoration for the whatnot or shelf.

Although the popularity of fairings waned after the war, Japanese porcelain makers found a ready market for these small china items in the United States and copies of German and British fairings can be found in abundance here. Most of these were made between the world wars, but some were made during the period of Allied occupation in Japan. Since many of these were made from molds designed from sample figures brought to Japan from England and Germany, the figures are not as well delineated and the features on the figures are not as carefully painted. Also, when two seemingly identical fairings—one made in Germany for the British market, the other a copy from Japan made for the American market—are compared, the Japanese copy will be slightly larger.

There were a great many souvenir items made for seaside visitors, but only the little porcelain objects are referred to as fairings by today's collector. Some of them are comic, some religious, and some carry titles or messages such as "Greetings from Brighton," but all have a kind of appeal that makes them as charming for collectors as they were for the original recipients.

FIESTA WARE

When the Homer Laughlin Company of Newell, West Virginia, introduced a line of mix-and-match dishes in Art Deco shapes and glazed in vibrant shades of red, blue, green, yellow, and ivory, its designers could not have predicted that they were starting a collecting trend which would include thousands of devotees. However, less than four decades after the line of dinnerware was introduced, the pattern, called Fiesta, is sought by people who attempt to put together entire sets of the dishes as well as all recorded serving pieces that were made. Fiesta was a popular pattern when it was first made, and Homer Laughlin continued to produce it until 1971.

Throughout the many years of production of Fiesta, many shapes and colors were introduced, so the variety available to present-day collectors is large enough to make this a fascinating collecting hobby. Two related patterns, Harlequin and Riviera, also made by Homer Laughlin, are collected along with Fiesta; enough research has been done by enthusiastic collectors and hobbyists to record what shapes and colors of all three of these patterns might be found. The plates and other shapes are easily identifiable, since the company marked all pieces with the pattern names. Because this style of dinnerware was commercially successful, other American pottery companies attempted to copy the Fiesta pattern and collectors are aware of these copies so that only "real" Fiesta is added to their collections.

During its long period of production, the Fiesta ware was so popular that at various times pieces in utilitarian kitchenware as well as giftware were added; today's collector can find mixing bowls as well as candleholders in the vibrant glazes. The pottery is collected so that place settings in each color

Fiesta ware relish tray, missing its center sauce dish, was made in the six original colors: yellow, blue, turquoise, red, green, and ivory. The shape was discontinued in 1945.

may be put together as a set. Some collectors search for one each of the many shapes that were made.

In today's scene of popular collectibles, Fiesta ware is a phenomenon in that its popularity appeared to spring up almost overnight. One reason for this is that it is a pattern that had great appeal for those involved in collecting Depression glass. After some wrangling, the Homer Laughlin pottery became "acceptable" as a salable item in Depression glass shows. Unless a show is advertised as *"All* Glass," people in search of additions to their Fiesta collections can usually find at least one dealer with ample supplies of Homer Laughlin pottery at the many Depression glass shows held throughout the country with great frequency.

Although it is far from "antique," Fiesta stirs a feeling of great nostalgia among to-

Stick-handled creamer was original Fiesta style. After 1941, creamers had more conventional ring handle. Fiesta sugar bowl is missing dome-shaped lid.

day's pottery collectors. Almost everyone knew or was related to someone who was an original owner of the pattern in the Thirties, Forties, and Fifties. Fiesta, designed by

British potter Fredrick Rhead, and modeled by Arthur Kraft and Bill Bersford, has tremendous popular appeal and is an American collectible with many followers.

PERIODICALS:

The Glaze
Haf-a-Productions
P. O. Box 4929 GS
Springfield, Missouri 65807

The National Glass, Pottery
*   *& Collectibles Journal*
1728 West Brower Street
Springfield, Missouri 65802

Note: See listings under Depression glass.

BOOKS:

The Collectors Encyclopedia of Fiesta, with Harlequin and Riviera, Sharon and Bob Huxford. Order from authors, Dept. DD, 1202 7th Street, Covington, Indiana 47932.

FRUIT JARS
AND FOOD
BOTTLES

The collecting of fruit and other preserving jars for food is an offshoot of bottle collecting, but it has become such a popular specialty that it is a category with its own history and appeal. The history of the development of the preservation of food in glass jars is one that begins in the first decade of the nineteenth century, and collectors are aware of the many changes and variations in the manufacture of fruit jars throughout the entire century.

Fruit jars were made for sale in the United States by Thomas W. Dyott as early as 1829. While the jars, themselves, did not change in shape very much, various people worked on the invention of better closures throughout the 1800s. John L. Mason, a tinsmith, was the first to develop a zinc screw lid, but other inventors continued to search for safer, more convenient ways of closing and sealing jars of preserved food.

Today's collectors search for jars with unusual closures, jars of unusual color, and especially for jars with embossed lettering that tells who made the jar and usually when it was patented. Although most fruit jars were made in clear glass in various shades of aqua, there are some rarities in opalescent glass, the fairly common amber, and the rarely found colors of green, cobalt blue, and milk glass. Pottery jars of the late nineteenth century can also be found.

Fruit jar collectors learn the history of home and commercial canning and, along with their jars and closures, collect early cookbooks with recipes used for food preservation, crates used for jars, early advertisements that are crucial to the history of their collecting area, and the great variety of tools once used in home canning.

Related to fruit jar collecting, but often a separate collecting area within the bottle collecting world, is the collecting of commercial food bottles. This is a more interesting collectible for many, who feel that fruit jars are too much alike. These specialists search for early bottles that once held pepper sauce and pickles. There are many fascinating shapes to look for, but perhaps the most appealing is the gothic style pickle bottle in shades of green ranging from very pale aqua to dark green. Occasionally, cathedral bottles are found in amber. Pepper sauce bottles, small and often with handsome embossed designs, are also in demand, especially if they are in colors other than light aqua. There are many other food jars that are sought by collectors. If they are early (made before 1920), of an interesting shape or color, or have embossments that indicate the maker and what the bottle once held, they are welcome additions to the collector's shelf.

Glass containers used for the preservation of food in the pre-plastic era are desirable as collector's items. They provide a relatively inexpensive way for collectors to become part of the varied bottle-collecting hobby that has grown so quickly across the country within the past decade.

Group of canning jars with variety of patented closures.

PERIODICALS AND CLUBS:

See "Bottles."

BOOKS:

A Collector's Guide to Ball Jars, William F. Brantley. Order from Ball Corporation, Direct Marketing Products, Muncie, Indiana 47302.

Fruit Jar Manual and Price Guide, Frank Peters. Old Bottle Magazine, Box 243, Bend, Oregon 97701.

Red Book of Fruit Jars, Alice M. Creswick. Order from author, 0-8525 Kenowa, S.W., Grand Rapids, Michigan 49504.

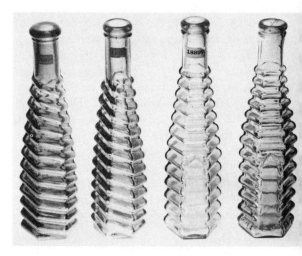

Group of pepper sauce bottles made in the nineteenth century.

Embossed food bottle of "The Great Atlantic and Pacific Tea Company."

The square milk bottle is a collector's item.

HAVILAND CHINA

Franklin Pierce ordered a set. As soon as she was comfortably ensconced in the White House, Mary Todd Lincoln ordered her china pattern from David Haviland in New York. Mrs. Ulysses S. Grant ordered her Haviland china decorated with buff borders, the presidential coat of arms, and flowers of America as the central decoration. The most unusual china service made for the White House was ordered by Mrs. Rutherford B. Hayes; sixteen artists worked on the designs and decoration. Reproductions of these patterns made expressly for use in the White House have been issued from time to time by Haviland and White House china is, perhaps, the most prestigious of all collector's plates. Many collectors are not aware that some of the presidential patterns are genuine. Until the Kennedy administration, part dinner sets and odd plates were often sold to second-hand dealers or at auction.

David Haviland was a New York importer of English china from 1839 who, in 1842, set up a factory in Limoges, France. He was impressed with the whiteness and quality of the china being made in that area of France and adapted English shapes and decoration to French chinaware. He also established methods of manufacture that were, for the time, modern; these were of an assembly-line nature that revolutionized French porcelain manufacture. Charles Field Haviland, David's nephew, looked after the business in France from around 1850 until 1880, while David ran the New York importing and decorating part of the business. Theodore Haviland, David's son, built his own factory in 1892 and, under the Haviland name, the New York firm and the Limoges works presently operate. The firm now produces chinaware in both countries.

All of the publicity accorded to Haviland, especially during the period when Theodore Haviland began his association with the firm, helped to create a huge American market for the fine, white china. Especially useful was the Hayes order for the unique designs. Haviland capitalized on this publicity by publishing a book describing how the Hayes service was made. Because the set was so expensive to produce, Haviland entered into an agreement with Mrs. Hayes that the designs could be reproduced and sold to the public after the original set was delivered. Pieces from this unique dinner service are still displayed and used in the White House.

The Haviland firm made sets of dishes for the American market from 1842 and continues to do so to this day. The fine, white vitreous body and high glaze of Haviland and the delicate, usually floral decoration of late nineteenth-century plates had strong appeal to American brides. There were a great many shapes and types of decoration from which to choose. Patterns of old Haviland found today range from neo-classic, through high Victorian, to Art Deco, Art Nouveau, and modern. Presently, Haviland also makes collector's series. Some of these series are in limited editions, numbered and signed, and are among the few collector's series of plates that may possibly increase in value with time.

During the country's Centennial celebration, Haviland reproduced the Lincoln, Pierce, and Grant plates with the back-

Two examples of Haviland plates, both shown front and back. The first is a Haviland Limoges, Martha Washington plate, and bears Haviland's signature. The first fifteen states of the United States circle the rim of the second plate.

stamp "Administration 'U.S. Grant'" or whatever administration had ordered the pattern. For the Bicentennial another series of presidential plates was issued in limited editions of five thousand each. Other series of decorated plates, made more for display than use, are continuously being made for the American market by Haviland. Expensive decorative china pieces for display are also produced from time to time, but dinnerware services remain the greater part of Haviland's business.

There are thousands of collectors of Haviland china in America. Many of today's collectors started their collections by inheriting a part dinner service, while others have purchased a few plates and have added to their sets from time to time. Cups and saucers, chocolate sets, butter pats, and covered serving dishes are shapes in which many collectors specialize.

Matching Haviland patterns has been simplified for collectors by Arlene Schleiger, who has written a series of books which identify the patterns by number. This series of five books is indispensable to collectors, who may order pieces in their pattern through the mail (see the chapter on Matchmakers in Part I).

Ms. Schleiger's books may be ordered by mail. The price for each book is $6.95; the cost is $29.95 for the series (postpaid). The address is:

Two Hundred Patterns of Haviland China
Arlene Schleiger
4416 Valli Vista Road
Colorado Springs, Colorado 80915

HEISEY GLASS

Glass collectors tend to specialize in more categories than any other collectors of American decorative arts. Perhaps that is because glass has always been a successful product in this country and the history of American glass is long and complicated. One group of collectors searches for the glass made from 1895 to 1954 by A. H. Heisey & Co. in Newark, Ohio. The company made both blown and pressed glass. Since most of the pressed glass and some of the blown glass was marked with the company's well-known trademark, an "H" in a diamond, the glass is easy to identify. Further identification has been facilitated by the reprinting of the company's old catalogs.

Within the total output of the Heisey firm there are many areas for further specialization. Some collectors search for blown and etched stemware, while others want only the useful pressed tableware. Others specialize in crystal and flashed ruby glass or the opaque, hand-painted glass known as "ivornina verde." The great variety of patterns, shapes, and art styles popular over the long period Heisey was in business are familiar to all Heisey collectors who haunt flea markets, antique shows, and glass shows in search of the glass.

Of special interest to most Heisey collectors are the simple shapes and patterns of the company's first quarter century. These pressed glass patterns include tumblers, coasters, plates, stemware, custard cups, finger bowls, bedroom sets (which include tankard, tray, candlestick, and matchbox or match striker), punch sets, cruets, and a long list of other shapes. Along with these useful objects in simple patterns, Heisey also made elaborate epergnes and candelabra.

Heisey collectors are interested in the history of the company and acquisition is only a part of this collecting scene. There is a lot to learn about the huge variety of patterns, shapes, and colors produced by this company, and Heisey collectors have been responsible for the great amount of research that has been done.

Heisey glass finger bowl and melon-shaped pitcher are both marked with "H" in diamond.

CLUBS:

Heisey Collectors of America, Inc.
P. O. Box 27
Newark, Ohio 43055

Note: A monthly publication, *Heisey News,* is one benefit of membership.

Heisey "Criss-cross" pattern bowl, marked with company's "H" in diamond, is a rarity.

Heisey goose in solid glass. This shape, with wings half up, is collector's item.

Heisey pressed glass, footed, covered compote is in rare "Zodiac" pattern.

Duncan and Miller glass, often collected by Heisey and Cambridge collectors, can be found in several swan shapes. Among the rarities are these solid or "fat-back" swans.

Fenton Burmese overlay glass vase with tooled, ruffled rim is the type of collectible wanted by those who appreciate fine American decorative glass.

Fenton glass, such as this milk glass vase in "Empress" pattern, is becoming as popular among collectors as Heisey, Cambridge, Duncan and Miller.

HUMMEL
FIGURINES

The number of Hummel collectors has grown recently. Demand has pushed up prices for all the Hummels made in the past.

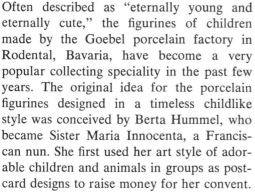

Often described as "eternally young and eternally cute," the figurines of children made by the Goebel porcelain factory in Rodental, Bavaria, have become a very popular collecting speciality in the past few years. The original idea for the porcelain figurines designed in a timeless childlike style was conceived by Berta Hummel, who became Sister Maria Innocenta, a Franciscan nun. She first used her art style of adorable children and animals in groups as postcard designs to raise money for her convent.

Goebel then asked to translate these designs into three-dimensional figurines made for the gift market and the convent became the recipient of royalties on the sales of the figures. The figure groups, which also include some religious groups, became popular gift items and collectibles almost from the start and at their original cost of from one to three dollars, many were purchased, especially in the United States, which imported many of them. Hummel figures were a natural collectible since their first production in the early 1930s. Although they are still being made, the price has increased to about thirty dollars.

It is the secondary and subsequent markets that are of more interest to collectors of Hummels, however. Collectors search for the figure groups that were made in small quantity, such as the one produced in 1935 and titled "Silent Night With Black Child." Another rarity is "Adoration With Bird." These rarities and others, when they can be found, bring high prices on today's market, since there are thousands of Hummel devotees, all of whom want the prestige of owning the rare pieces.

Hummel figures, although not antique, have great appeal for many. This is a relatively "new" popular collectible that is easy to date and study; interest in these figures will undoubtedly continue for a long time to come.

Schmid Brothers of Massachusetts was Goebel's designated importer to America from the mid-1930s until 1967, when Goebel decided to do its own distribution and cancelled Schmid's contract. Schmid then bought rights from the family of Sister Berta for some drawings they still owned. Until this time, only the convent had profited from the rights to Sister Berta's art. Hummelware under the Schmid name appeared on the American market and lawsuits for renewal of copyrights, as well as related countersuits, continue. Meanwhile, collector's plates made by both Goebel and Schmid appear on the market with some regularity. Collectors generally agree that the Goebel products are higher quality, but all are aware that anything made before 1967 is genuine Hummelware.

In addition to the above dispute and the knowledge that two companies have used Sister Berta's original drawings and art style, there are some Japanese imitations of Hummel figurines made before and after World War II. These are of inferior quality, are marked, and should cause no confusion for the knowledgeable collector.

In general, collectors search for the older editions of figurines; prices for these have begun to soar. What was inexpensive popular art for several decades has now become a group of expensive collector's items to the more than fifty thousand American collectors who love Hummel figurines.

CLUBS:

Goebel Collectors Club
105 White Plains Road
Tarrytown, New York 10591

BOOKS:

Hummel, The Complete Collector's Guide and Illustrated Reference, Eric Ehrmann. Portfolio Press, Huntington, New York 11743.

Hummel Art, John Hotchkiss. Hotchkiss House, 181 Hearthstone Road, Pittsford, New York 14534.

INKWELLS AND INKSTANDS

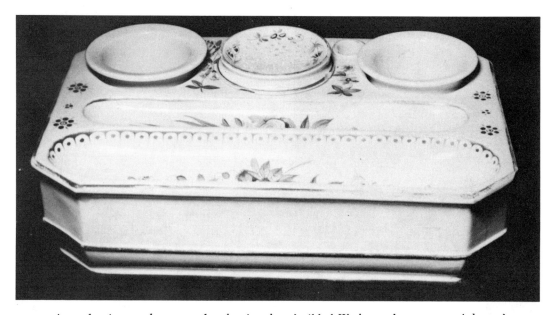

An early nineteenth-century hand-painted and gilded Wedgwood creamware inkstand.

Whether you prefer the rococo style of the early eighteenth century or the plain colonial period of decoration, there are inkwells made over a period of several centuries that are worth collecting. Most inkwell collectors search for all decorative ink containers that were made in the past. The variety in style, material, and decoration makes this collecting hobby one that is never-ending.

There are many ways of specializing in the collecting of inkwells and inkstands. Collectors might search only for glass inkwells and amass a huge collection over the years. Other collectors purchase only pottery and porcelain inkwells: such a collection might include examples from the finest European potters as well as handsome Chinese or Japanese containers. It would be

possible to purchase only inkwells made by Wedgwood in the eighteenth and nineteenth century and still have a fair-size collection.

A comprehensive collection of inkwells will include all of the decorative styles used in past centuries in almost all of the countries of the world. Examples of the finest work of early glassblowers, silvermakers, or pewterers can be represented by inkwells, and the necessity for some type of reservoir for ink on every desk in every house led to the making of the most elaborate desk appurtenances as well as homemade, simple containers.

Travel inkwells can be found that are simple, small containers with tight-fitting tops. The ultimate in traveling inkwells were the desk boxes that were usually fitted

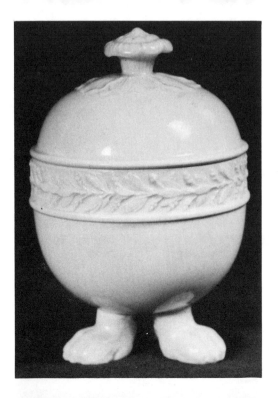

Wedgwood creamware inkwell, made in three parts, was designed to control the level of ink.

Drab-colored glaze, gilding, and elaborate design place this inkstand in the mid-nineteenth century.

with at least two removable wells. These were often made of crystal with silver screw-caps.

Within the category of inkwell collecting, the possibilities are almost limitless if one's funds are equally without bottom. Because so many inkwells were made over such a long period of time, there are still many available. Collectors search for the exqui-site, the unusual, or sometimes for presentation pieces that have historical connections.

BOOKS:

Inkwells and Inkstands, Betty and Ted Rivera. Crown Publishers, Inc., One Park Avenue, New York, New York 10016.

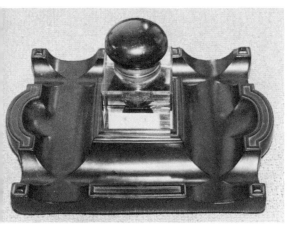

Mission-style bronze inkstand was made at end of last century.

Leather-covered traveling inkwell made by Waterman Ink Company.

Nineteenth-century glass inkwell.

Openwork silver inkstand.   *Barrel-shaped wooden inkwell with screw top designed for travel.*

INSULATORS

Armstrong's No. 2 is one of many shapes, colors, and sizes to be found in this type of glass and pottery collectible.

They're called "Pole Cats" and, although it's dangerous and illegal, there are some insulator collectors who have been known to obtain their best specimens of insulators by climbing old telephone poles and plucking the coveted hunks of glass from them. Mostly, collectors find insulators in old dumps, along the sides of roads, or in junk shops. Many let others find them; they then buy them at flea markets and bottle or insulator shows.

The glass cups and other innovative shapes were developed after the telegraph made its debut in 1844. Later, after 1876, when the telephone came into use, many more insulators were needed. Prized items are threadless insulators made between 1850 and 1870. There is a great variety of sizes and shapes, with the largest made by Pyrex. It weighed 38 pounds. Porcelain insulators came on the scene during World War II and made glass insulators obsolete and, therefore, collector's items. Shapes, embossings, and the variety of glass colors are all qualities that determine rarity and price. Embossments reveal the names of the manufacturers and patent dates and the list of glassmakers in the business is almost endless.

More than 3,500 different shapes and types of glass insulators have been found and recorded in this hobby that once attracted people who were employees of telephone companies and to whom the collecting hobby appealed because of their special interest. The collectors are students of the American glass industry, although some have branched out into collecting insulators from all over the world.

BOOKS:

Rare Insulators with Prices, Frances Terrill. The Terrills, 2356 N.W. Quimby Street, Portland, Oregon 97210.

JOHN ROGERS GROUPS

Originally there were more than eighty thousand of the cast plaster figures and figure groups made by the popular sculptor, John Rogers, between 1860 and 1893. P. T. Barnum called them "one of the wonders of the age." At the time, the average price for one of Rogers' sculptures was fourteen dollars; today, one might sell for many thousands. In between their original popularity and today's eager collector, the sculpture was relegated to attics and basements along with tons of other Victorian clutter.

Rogers' work was sold throughout the country and there are collectors everywhere who search for examples of the realistic groups sculptured by the artist. His work has been described as folk art or fine art, but it has great appeal for the many enthusiasts who are responsible for its survival. Rogers groups represent figures of average folks doing things common to all middle-class Americans in the nineteenth century. They were made to appeal to these same people (and priced accordingly) and they are extremely well detailed, with the characters in realistic poses. "Neighboring Pews" and "Checkers up at the Farm" are two examples of the lively realism Rogers was able to achieve. His seated statuette of Abraham Lincoln reading a document is well known and in great demand among collectors, as is his 1864 statuette of a young Black man leading a wounded Civil War scout.

There are not a great many Rogers groups in hiding anymore. Dealers and collectors have been advertising for years for the groups in any condition. There is always the possibility, however, that yet one more little old lady will clean out her attic and come across the statue that used to sit on the table in the parlor and that she will want to part with it. Barring that, however, there are reproductions of Rogers statuary presently being produced in limited editions of 650 each in bronze. An investment in one of these costs more than one would have had to spend to buy all of John Rogers' work at its original price!

John Rogers Commemorative Society, Inc.
275 Route 18
East Brunswick, New Jersey 08816

Sells Rogers groups in limited editions of 650 made by lost wax process.
First group, "Checkers up at the Farm."
Membership includes appraisal service for Rogers groups and memorabilia, bimonthly newsletters.
Purchase not necessary.

John Rogers group, "Neighboring Pews."

Rogers group, "Checkers up at the Farm."

KITCHEN COLLECTIBLES

Butter molds were made in a great number of folk art designs.

Flea markets and the merchandise found in them are usually indications of what the next popular collectible will be. Recently, more and more dealers are specializing in old kitchen items. These are not the hand-made wooden implements of past centuries, but manufactured items that were new only forty or fifty years ago. Now that La Machine has replaced "la tin grater" and orange juice is "squeezed" from paper cartons, the old grater and the glass juice reamers are in demand as collectible artifacts worth displaying in country-style kitchens. There is at least one antique dealer who specializes in rolling pins.

Old wooden butter mold is a desirable kitchen collectible.

Carved wood kitchen utensils, such as these made by the Shakers, are desirable collectibles regardless of their condition.

Tin dipper, a handsome country kitchen collectible.

English glass lemon reamer has patent date of 1888. There are people who specialize in collecting old citrus fruit reamers of all types and sizes.

All kitchen gadgets of pre-World War I vintage are being collected. This was a Wesson Oil giveaway for making mayonnaise.

Any metal, glass, or ceramic item that was once used in the kitchen barely one generation ago—if it has been replaced by plastic or if it looks old-fashioned—is wanted by collectors for their kitchens. Some of these items are once again put to the use for which they were intended. Huge pottery mixing bowls and heavy black iron skillets are still convenient and utilitarian, and they don't make them today the way they used to. Large breadboards of seasoned wood are more convenient than plastic or fiber-glass slabs, and tin measuring cups will not break.

Mostly, kitchen collectibles are used as decoration. The laboratory type of kitchen that was once popular has gone out of style and kitchens are decorated today as family centers. Old baskets are in great demand as wall decoration and the sun shines through collections of colored glass refrigerator dishes, citrus fruit reamers, and measuring cups that were made in the 1920s and Thirties. These are often displayed on window shelves in many collectors' kitchens.

Old crocks, measuring scoops, wooden food containers, tin containers, or anything that might have been found in your grandmother's or mother's kitchen is probably worth keeping and displaying today. All old commercial food packaging, as well as advertising items connected to products no longer being marketed or products that are marketed differently, have value to someone. Tin biscuit boxes, especially those with nostalgic decoration, are in such demand that they have become an area of specialization for some collectors. Many are being reproduced.

No one needs to be reminded that the grocery store giveaways of yesteryear are highly collectible today. Many of these fall into the realm of Depression glass or collectible pottery. Food items such as maple syrup, vinegar, and tea have, in the past, been sold in decorative containers that were "keepers" and are now desirable collector's items.

Like peanuts, the ownership of one set of "cute" figural salt-and-pepper-shaker sets led to the desire for more for housewives of the 1930s and Forties, and there are thousands of these ceramic, glass, wood, or metal sets around today. Most of these, but certainly not all, were made in Japan before and after World War II; they were made more for collecting than for practical use. Many were of fragile design, such as the figure of a Pullman porter precariously holding salt-and-pepper suitcases in either hand, or painted pottery canoes with removable salt-and-pepper Indians. There are many second-time-around collectors of these colorful sets and the prime items among them are those marked "Made in Occupied Japan." These nostalgic and decorative kitchen items can be found at garage sales, flea markets, and tag sales, but the price today is usually a lot higher than the original ten cents or a quarter.

Like toys, kitchen collectibles don't have to be very old to be worth buying. Many new collectors have recently become enchanted with the many categories of old kitchen items by inheriting unusual gadgets of the past such as a glass rolling pin that was made to be filled with ice water for perfect piecrust or a handsome nest of three cobalt blue mixing bowls marked "Hazel Atlas." The inheritance of a few of grandmother's old kitchen tools frequently leads to the search for more kitchen items, which seem to continue to go up in value each year.

CLUBS:

Shakers International
2925 18th Street
Greeley, Colorado 80631

This is a salt-and-pepper-shaker collectors' club.

BOOKS:

American Kitchen Collectibles, Identification and Price Guide, Mary Lou Matthews. L-W Promotions, Box 69, Gas City, Indiana 46933.

Antique American Wall Match Holders, Betty H. Rimalover. Stoneybrook Associates, Box 11, Princeton Junction, New Jersey 08550.

Antique Household Gadgets and Appliances c. 1860–1930, David de Haan. Barron's Educational Series, Inc., 113 Crossways Park Drive, Woodbury, New York 11797.

Collecting Old Granite-Ware, Porcelain-on-Steel: A Forerunner of Aluminum Kitchenware, edited by Larry Freeman. Century House, Watkins Glen, New York 14891.

A Collector's Guide to Pressing Irons and Trivets, Esther S. Berney. Crown Publishers, Inc., One Park Avenue, New York, New York 10016.

From Hearth to Cookstove, Linda Campbell Franklin. House of Collectibles, Florence, Alabama 356.

Kitchenware, Geraldine Cosentino and Regina Stewart. Western Publishing Company, Inc., 850 Third Avenue, New York, New York 10022.

Stoneware: A Guide for the Beginning Collector, Regina Stewart and Geraldine Cosentino. Golden Press, Western Publishing Company, Inc., 850 Third Avenue, New York, New York 10022.

Tuesday's Children, Collecting Little Irons and Trivets, Judy and Frank Politzer. Order from the authors, 50 Layman Court, Walnut Creek, California 94596.

LIMITED EDITION COLLECTORS' PLATES

Plate, made for Wedgwood Collectors Society, entitled "Chief Black Hawk, Sauk and Fox Tribes, 1767–1838," was issued in a limited edition of 5,000 in 1971.

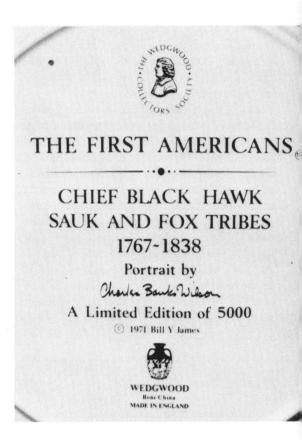

THE FIRST AMERICANS

CHIEF BLACK HAWK
SAUK AND FOX TRIBES
1767-1838
Portrait by
Charles Banks Wilson
A Limited Edition of 5000
© 1971 Bill Y James

WEDGWOOD
Bone China
MADE IN ENGLAND

Limited edition plates are a phenomenon of the current collecting field. Huge numbers of people wait breathlessly for the new editions of plates manufacturers produce annually for the purpose of collecting and displaying. These plates may be glass, porcelain, pottery, or silver; they are usually designed or decorated by well-known, popular artists. Prices range from a few dollars to several hundreds of dollars. Collecting in this area requires little or no special knowledge unless one is also a dealer or speculator.

Most special editions of collectors' plates are issued for a particular holiday and are purchased annually by gift givers who solve their problems of what to select for Christmas, Mother's Day, or some other holiday for as long as the series continues. In the

HISTORICAL CANADIAN VESSELS
'H.M.S. DISCOVERY'

BUILT IN THE YARD OF RANDALL & BRENT ON THE
THAMES IN 1789, AND PURCHASED BY THE ROYAL NAVY
AS A SUITABLE VESSEL FOR USE IN EXPLORATION

L.O.A. 99 ft. 2 ins.   BEAM ABOUT 30 ft.
DISPLACEMENT 330 tons.

SHE WAS RIGGED AS A SHIP AND CARRIED 10 FOUR
POUNDERS AND 10 SWIVELS

H.M.S. DISCOVERY WAS COMMANDED BY CAPTAIN
GEORGE VANCOUVER IN HIS GREAT WORK OF EXPLOR-
ING AND CHARTING THE COAST OF NORTH-WEST
AMERICA IN 1791-1795

WHILE ON THIS VOYAGE CAPTAIN VANCOUVER
SAILED H.M.S. DISCOVERY INTO " DE FUCA'S SUPPOSED
STRAITS " AND TO THE PRESENT SITE OF THE CITY OF
VANCOUVER, B.C.

DESIGNED AND DRAWN BY ROWLEY MURPHY, A.R.C.A., O.S.A.
(OFFICIAL ROYAL CANADIAN NAVAL WAR ARTIST.)

"H.M.S. Discovery" plate is part of a series of Historical Canadian Vessels designed
for Wedgwood by Rowley Murphy.

case of plates made by Bing and Grondahl, the gift-giving problem has been solved for some since 1895. Royal Copenhagen has been issuing limited edition plates annually since 1908. However, the contemporary scene of limited edition plates really got started around 1970 and has grown to enormous proportions since then.

There is little doubt that the market in contemporary collectors' plates is a contrived one, with speculators buying up first issues and holding them to boost the original investment. Most editions are limited only to what can be produced in the year before the next plate is issued. Figures as to exactly how limited such an edition really is are seldom, if ever, released by the manufacturers. A few special series have been made, such as Haviland's Bicentennial reproductions of White House china, where the series is truly limited to a certain number, but this is the exception rather than the rule. One has only to visit the gift departments of discount stores to see the large number of leftover Christmas or Mother's Day plates made by Wedgwood or other

firms that were not sold out and are then sold at discounted prices. This would lead one to believe that most limited edition collectors' plates are fine to buy or display but should certainly never be purchased as an investment. Stories circulate about certain editions of collector's series selling at prices far above their original cost, but this is the rare exception rather than the rule. Usually, this happens in a series where the first plate issued was made in a smaller amount than subsequent issues and popularity of later issues creates a desire for all plates in the series.

The market for collectors' plates is enormous, and producers have chosen as plate decorations every possible subject that can be continued as a series—from biblical themes to "Whistler's Mother" (and subsequent other famous paintings). Plate makers manage to come up with more and newer "works of art" each month. Many of the series are sold through the mail, making it even easier to become an instant "collector." There are also specialist dealers who keep their customers aware of each new

LEFT: *Bing and Grondahl plates produced annually at Christmas time since 1895 are among the few collector's plate series that may go up in value.*
RIGHT: *Limited edition plates made of Limoges porcelain are a series of six with colorful motifs derived from Flemish tapestries.*

issue from each manufacturer. Expensive mailings keep the collector apprised of what's new in plates. Many of our contemporary journals on antiques and collecting are largely supported by advertising from the manufacturers of limited edition plates. Therefore, articles extolling the virtues of each new edition of plates proliferate and, so far, the market in limited edition collectors' plates has been growing.

If plates decorated with prints by Edna Hibel or Norman Rockwell are satisfying decorations in your living room, by all means continue to wait for the next one. For collectors who find the search most of the fun in collecting, limited editions of new plates, sent automatically through the mail, are of no interest. There is little you have to know about this hobby except that you

should be wary in selecting the types of plates to collect. Unless you are a dealer, do not buy limited edition plates as an investment. Consider the plates as pleasant decoration for your home.

BOOKS:

Bradford Book of Collector's Plates. The Bradford Exchange, 8700 Waukegan Road, Morton Grove, Illinois 60053.

The Kovels' Collector's Guide to Limited Editions, Ralph and Terry Kovel. Crown Publishers, One Park Avenue, New York, New York 10016.

Plate Collecting, Eleanor Clark. Citadel Press, 120 Enterprise Avenue, Secaucus, New Jersey 07094.

LITHOPHANES

The process for molding translucent pictures into porcelain originated in Paris in 1827 and the inventor, Baron de Bouring, sold licenses for this novel way of treating porcelain to potters in Holland, England, and Germany. Lithophanes were made in small panels, used originally as plaques to be hung in windows, and later adapted as lampshade panels. German stein makers made lithophane scenes for the bottoms of their beer mugs. Once emptied of the brew, the mugs further delighted imbibers with scenes from Faust or views of Munich.

Lithophanes have been collector's items for many years. They were a popular art form in the nineteenth century, when craftsmen and artists searched for ways to adapt art to the mass production methods that were prevalent during the period. Although the making of molds for lithophanes was expensive and complicated, many lithophanes could be turned out from a single mold once the artist's work was finished.

Lithophanes had great appeal in the Victorian age and that appeal has carried over to thousands of collectors in this century. Because they are fragile, many of the panels broke or cracked, and not enough of the European lithophanes have survived to satisfy today's collectors. Those that do come on the market are often damaged and, if not, are quite expensive.

There are, however, lithophanes for today's collector that are still not prohibitively high in price. These were made in Japan for export to the West from around 1900 and the process continued to be used for about three decades into this century. Lithophanes made by the Japanese were used on the bottoms of porcelain teacups. Some of these imported porcelain tea sets

This Japanese tea set, with its heavy gilding and elaborate pattern, has lithophane cup bottoms.

will feature only one lithophane in a complete set of china. Other sets will have a lithophane in the base of each cup. The subject matter most often seen in Japanese lithophanes is a well-modeled portrait of a Japanese woman. Another subject, less often seen, is a full-length picture of two nude women with arms intertwined. The modeling is so carefully done, obviously by talented artists used to working in miniature, that the picture appears to be almost photographic when held to the light. Unless the teacup is held to the light, the picture cannot be seen at all and only a slight irregularity in the inside surface of the cup is evident.

Lithophane art, whether found on lampshades, inside beer steins, or at the base of a Japanese teacup, is a lost process. It was a

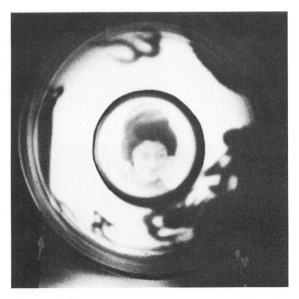

When light shines through the base of the teacups of the set on page 151, lithophane portrait of a Japanese woman appears to be almost photographic.

A lithophane portrait in the base of a porcelain teacup.

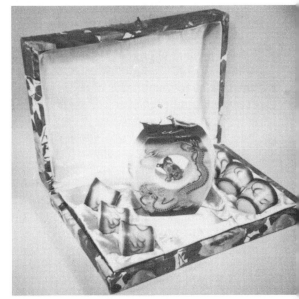

A decorative sake *set, made for the American market in the 1920s, has only one lithophane of a pair of nude women. The other cups are plain.*

complicated and tedious way for porcelain makers to sell their products. While the lithophanes of Minton, Copeland, or Wedgwood have been collected for a long time and are well known, today's collector is more apt to search for the more abundant Japanese novelty porcelains of this century with the secret pictures molded into them.

MADE IN OCCUPIED JAPAN

As prices for quality antiques and collectibles keep rising, many collectors of modest means search for interesting categories in which they can specialize, that they can afford, and that include a variety of objects that they can still find in some quantity. Objects made during a short time after World War II by the Japanese for export to the United States fill these requirements for thousands of new collectors. This is a made-to-order category of collecting for people with limited pocketbooks and a strong interest in popular decorative and useful objects.

Although the Allied occupation of Japan lasted from 1945 to 1952, most of these marked export pieces were made only during the latter four or five years of that period and represent an attempt by the Japanese to get their economy to a point where they would no longer be dependent upon their former enemies for support. Always an ingenious people, the Japanese made a great variety of goods for export. These consisted of objects made of porcelain, pottery, wood, glass, paper, metal, celluloid, cloth, and plastic and were mainly supplied to variety stores and low-priced department stores. An abbreviated list of items made would include toys, dolls, porcelain figurines, dishes, salt and pepper shakers, baby clothes, paintbrushes, kitchen novelties, ashtrays, paper and cloth fans, parasols, clocks, watches, cigarette lighters, cameras, binoculars, pincushions, needle books, measuring tapes, rulers, and countless other items. What these objects all have in common is that they were all, according to U. S. Customs regulations, marked "Occupied Japan" or "Made in Occupied Japan." Depending upon the material out of which the objects were made, there is some kind of identifying mark, either a stamp or a paper sticker, that tells you when, where, and under what unique circumstances the object was made. All of them represent a strange period in American-Japanese relationships.

A comprehensive collection of "Made in Occupied Japan" objects, the majority of which are porcelain figures designed and decorated in every national costume ever worn, will turn a shelf into a copy of a 1950s gift department of a chain variety store. These figurines were made to sell in a range of ten cents to a few dollars and do not, as a whole, represent anything close to fine art in porcelain production. Some are better quality than others, but most were considered, and indeed were made to be, cheap imitations of European decorative porcelain. Some are direct copies. The better quality of these are the bisque groups and single figures. Most figurines were made in boy-girl pairs and eighteenth-century costumes of Europe prevail in these pieces.

A category of "O.J." items that is highly prized by collectors is the huge variety of windup toys and dolls. While many were made, they were easily broken, and relatively few have survived. Marked glass items are scarce, as are the more ephemeral novelty items such as paper exploding ci-

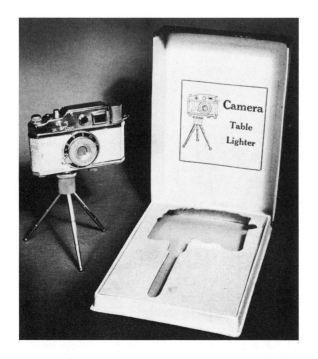

"Made in Occupied Japan" collectibles include a huge variety of objects, from table lighters that look like cameras to real working cameras.

gars, celluloid squirting lapel flowers, cloth and lace doilies, and miniature doll dishes. Most "Occupied Japan" items are small and easily displayed. The smallest—the miniature toys, dishes, and other objects—are in great demand.

Other items that are especially desirable and more expensive than the usual ten-cent-store items include clocks, bride and groom wedding cake ornaments, lamps, silk parasols and fans, and hand-carved wood figures. Complete sets of marked dinnerware, tea sets, and luncheon sets in certain patterns typical of Japanese ornament are also of interest to collectors.

"Made in Occupied Japan" collectors know that a search of a flea market or garage sale may turn up a slide rule or a cigarette lighter made to look like a miniature camera. The list of what has been found so far is almost endless and recent searches have brought to light a marked hand-hooked rug, excellent quality lacquerware, wooden salad sets, and bamboo stocking driers. This is a collecting hobby that's new, not too expensive, and full of surprises.

Souvenir ashtray and harmonica.

BOOKS:

Made in Occupied Japan: A Collector's Guide, Marian Klamkin. Crown Publishers, Inc., One Park Avenue, New York, New York 10016.

CLUBS:

Occupied Japan Collectors' Club
Robert W. Ree, Sr.
P. O. Box 6154
Torrance, California 90504

Above and right, strongly carved animal figure and fine handmade lacquer.

Copies of Hummel figures and copies of English printed pottery.

German-style bisque figurine made and decorated for the American market.

A pair of dolls usually made only for Japanese children's Doll Day.

"Made in Occupied Japan" spherical clock has a celluloid bird that turns back and forth with each tick.

MATCHBOOK COVERS

Collecting "railroads" is only one specialty in the inexpensive and satisfying matchbook cover hobby.

There's very little that's free these days, especially in a popular collecting field. Yet, there are thousands of collectors who amass huge groups of collectibles that they got for nothing. It's only the secondary market in matchbook covers that involves the exchange of hard cash and, even then, it's usually not a big investment. Nevertheless, there's a worldwide network of matchbook cover collectors who derive a great deal of enjoyment from their hobby.

There are unlimited ways in which a collector of matchbook covers can specialize. While many do have special areas of interest, others collect *all* unusual covers in order to trade off with others to get the covers they want. The hobby is called "phillumeny" and representative collections are a pop art history of this century. It is not unusual for a dedicated phillumenist to own more than a hundred thousand covers; these are divided and filed according to subject matter in shoe boxes, files, or albums. Some collectors have very specialized interests and collect only those covers that are representative of that specialty, whether it be one hotel or motel chain, shipping or railroad lines, or pictures of nude women. Other collectors search for local advertising covers of businesses in their own communities while others specialize in covers representing certain national or international products. Airlines and railroads are popular subjects.

While matchbook covers may be thought to be among the most disposable of paper items that are collected, the dedicated collectors are well aware that they are recording popular history by collecting the cardboard scraps in albums, trading off the unwanted for the desirable, and in some cases buying groups of covers already arranged for them in categories.

An advantage in collecting matchbook covers is that trading can be done easily through the mail. The hobby is well organized and there is a great deal of swapping among club members who are aware of each other's special interests. Mostly, collecting matchbook covers is fun for those involved, and it does involve thousands of people of all ages who search for the products of the three major American makers of book matches—Universal, Diamond, and Lion Match Corporation. As with any organized collectible, phillumenists have their own jargon, which describes the types of matchbooks that are made, and they keep track of each other through club newsletters.

CLUBS:

Rathkamp Matchcover Society
16283 Festian Drive
Fraser, Michigan 48026

Sunshine State Matchcover Club
  of Florida
222 Ranger Boulevard
Winter Park, Florida 32789

BOOKS:

Matchcovers: A Guidebook for Collectors, Esther Rancier. Century House, Inc., Watkins Glen, New York 14891.

MOTHER-OF-PEARL AND SEASHELLS

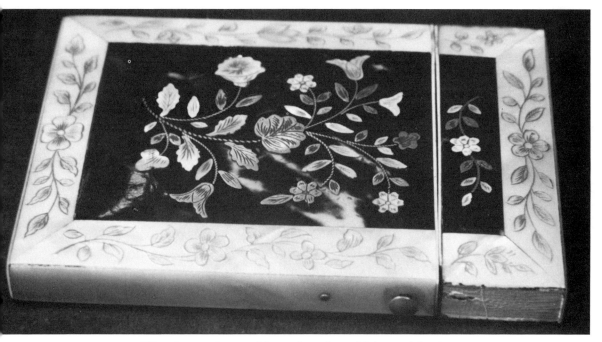

Victorian card case with mother-of-pearl inlay and border.

Mother-of-pearl, a gift from Mother Nature, was a favorite material used in the making of decorative objects through many centuries. Jewelry, card cases, flatware handles, knives, opera glasses, shell flowers, fans, and cups are only a few of the objects made from entire shells or pieces thereof. Buttons, of course, were made by the millions.

Seashells have been carved, set in silver or gold, and used to decorate furniture. Sailors, for centuries, found ways to use seashells as material for their handicrafts. Southwestern Native Americans still design superior contemporary jewelry using pieces of shells along with semiprecious stones. Shells have been used in the past in place of money.

Although there are thousands of collectors who like their shells whole and collect every variety they can find, there are others who are fascinated by the many ways in which man has adapted seashells to useful and decorative objects. Throughout the nineteenth century, artisans and decorators found myriad ways to incorporate shells in household objects. Most of the mother-of-pearl collectibles found today are from that

Papier mâché lady's compendium has elaborate mother-of-pearl ornamentation.

era, when the mass manufacture of decorative objects for the home reached its peak. There is hardly an auction of nineteenth-century household objects that does not include in its listings something made or inlaid with "M.O.P." Card cases, boxes, chairs, tables, wall plaques, and dishes were made in quantity and many collectors search for anything with bits of shimmery, iridescent shell from that era. Sailors' valentines, most of them made in Barbados and purchased by seamen as souvenirs, are a popular collectible for shell lovers and collectors of marine antiques. There are also one-of-a-kind engraved shells made in the same era as scrimshawed whalebone. A real find for a contemporary shell collector

Papier mâché box inlaid with mother-of-pearl.

An entire seashell was used as part of this Art Deco table decoration.

would be the tiny shells grouped to represent elaborate flower arrangements by some enterprising Victorian woman and preserved for posterity under a bell jar.

There are, of course, thousands of conchologists who prefer their shells uncut and in their natural form. They study the animal life of the sea and catalog and mount specimens; many amass huge collections. Some of our most complete museum collections were donations made by amateur conchologists, many of whom were able to travel the world to make their accumulations of seashells as complete as possible.

Whether one prefers seashells in their natural state or adapted in some way as decoration for home or person, there are many ways in which one might specialize. For instance, there are collectors who just look for mother-of-pearl snuffboxes or card cases. Others buy only the *hishe* jewelry of the Southwest or cameos of Italy. Anyone enamored of Victorian papier mâché production will inevitably own objects of that material with designs or pictures made of inlaid mother-of-pearl. There are always admirers of luster and iridescence. When these qualities are to be found in a material as varied and handsome as seashells, many people will admire it and collect objects made with such elements.

NEEDLEWORK AND SEWING DEVICES

Collecting all of the sewer's and embroiderer's paraphernalia of the past is a broad field that includes a great many possibilities for specialization. It is a hobby that can be as expensive or as inexpensive as will suit the pocketbook of the collector, and it can be pursued by someone who lives in a three-room apartment, though it offers specializations that will quickly fill a mansion if they are pursued with any vigor.

Perhaps the most popular specialty within the category of sewing and needlework devices is thimble collecting. Thimbles have been used as long as the needle has, and they have been made in a great many materials, decorated with almost every possible design. As a category with almost unlimited possibilities, thimble collecting is an old hobby with many enthusiasts. Therefore, manufacturers have made thimbles especially for collectors and special new "limited edition" thimbles are still offered with some regularity. The search goes on, however, for unusual or decorative thimbles that were made in the past to be used. Hand-painted porcelain, silver, gold, or enameled thimbles of the eighteenth and nineteenth centuries are the prizes in such collections and can be categorized today as fine antique jewelry. Frequently, these old and valuable thimbles are part of tiny sewing kits made to hang from chatelaines that were attached to gold chains and tucked into one's belt. The thimble collector does not purchase only the gems of the hobby, but searches for unusual thimbles once used by tailors and seamstresses.

Sewing compendia, owned by all proper ladies one and two centuries ago, are prime collectibles in the category of sewing devices. Boxes fitted out with scissors, needle books, thimbles, and other tools of the trade could be small and easy to carry, or they could be large and have extra drawers and secret compartments for scent, makeup, writing paper, and whatever else a woman might want to keep together in one storage or travel case. These boxes were made in every possible material, from papier mâché to Wedgwood-inlaid rosewood. When one is found for sale today with its original fittings, it is a desirable item for collectors of sewing devices.

Lacemaking bobbins, crochet hooks, knitting needles, embroidery hoops and stands, and all the other appurtenances of needlework are desirable collectibles. Pincushions, made in every possible configuration, are a collecting category in themselves. High on every pincushion collector's list are the pincushion dolls, those porcelain half-figures who had stuffed fabric skirts, a convenient place to stick pins and needles.

A revival of handicrafts has taken the old spinning wheel out of the parlor, where it was once considered a decorative accessory for colonial furniture, and missing parts have been restored to make the old wheels functional. Old looms have also been restored, and revivalists of the arts of spinning and weaving search for shuttles, recipes for vegetable dye, and instructions with patterns. Included in this interest is the desire for all the tools of linen-making, among them carders and hatchels.

The products of eighteenth- and nine-

Signed and dated pieced quilt in star pattern.

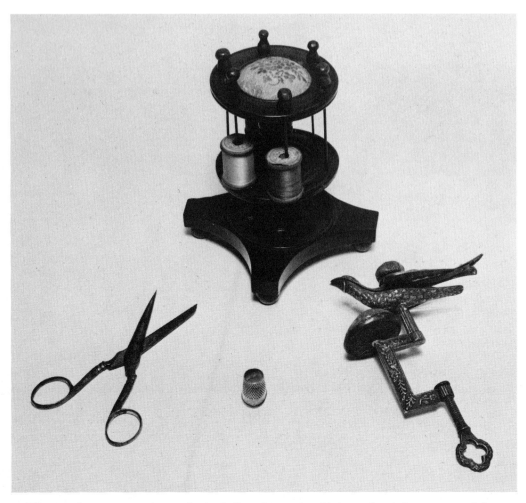

Nineteenth-century sewing tools, including the sewing bird on the right, are prized by collectors.

teenth-century needleworkers also are restored and collected today. Samplers made by children in the past have long been desirable collector's items, but it has only been for the past quarter of a century that woven coverlets and old quilts have had a lot of attention from dealers and collectors. The crocheted and tatted antimacassars that once protected every surface in the house are again revered, although presently they are more apt to be framed behind glass than they are to be used on the arms of overstuffed chairs. Bits of old handmade lace and embroidery are treasured by some collectors, who are aware that these forms of household art have all but disappeared.

All of the old tools used to produce the needlework of the past, as well as the products made by their use, are highly desired by today's collector. Included in this category are the objects that made the fine art of hand needlework obsolete. In recent years, there has been a growing number of enthusiasts who search for, restore, and save all examples of old sewing machines that they can find. Many of the early sewing machines were as handsome as they were practical. Collectors want, especially, those machines designed to appeal visually. They were hand-lined in gold, inlaid with mother-of-pearl, and sometimes set in handsome, polished wood cases. These are graceful mechanical devices that changed the civilized world in the last quarter of the nine-

Shaker-made sewing stand has pincushion, needle book, beeswax, and thread spool.

Sewing box from last century is also a music box that plays when opened.

teenth century, and they are simple enough to restore to working order by the collector who enjoys a challenge.

Whether one collects the tools or the products of those tools, needlework and sewing devices lead to a knowledge of the history of textiles and domestic and personal fashion. Collections today can include items as ephemeral as needle books and as sturdy as an old oak-encased Singer.

CLUBS:

Collector Circle
150-11 14th Avenue
Whitestone, New York 11357

The Thimble Guilde
Evelyn Eubanks
315 Park End Drive
Dayton, Ohio 45415

BOOKS:

American Hooked and Sewn Rugs, Joel and Kate Kopp. E. P. Dutton, 201 Park Avenue South, New York, New York 10003.

New Discoveries in American Quilts, Robert Bishop. E. P. Dutton, 201 Park Avenue South, New York, New York 10003.

Pincushions, Averil Colby. Charles Scribner's Sons, 597 Fifth Avenue, New York, New York 10017.

Textile Collector's Guide, Else Sommer. Simon and Schuster, 1230 Avenue of the Americas, New York, New York 10020.

Thimbles, Edwin F. Holmes. Sewing Corner, Inc., 150-11 14th Avenue, Whitestone, New York 11357.

Veteran Sewing Machines, A Collector's Guide, F. Brian Jewell. A. S. Barnes & Company, Inc., Box 421, Cranbury, New Jersey 08512.

A Winterthur Guide to American Needlework, Susan Burrows Swan. Crown Publishers, Inc., One Park Avenue, New York, New York 10016.

Leather-covered box has manicure and mending tools.

"Little man" silk pincushions were made in China in the 1920s, and are once again being exported.

Needle book, depicting Occidental family in an airplane, was made in Occupied Japan.

NODDERS

Hand and head of this porcelain nodder move when touched. The motion continues for a minute or so.

Touch its head and for a full minute this small porcelain figure with its inscrutable expression will shake its head negatively. Its limp hand will gesture "go away" for an equal length of time when it is set in motion. Nodding figurines were made to make you smile, and that's the main reason they were so popular in the last half of the nineteenth century.

Nodders are a category of collecting that has become popular during the past decade with people for whom static figurines are boring. Although they probably originated with the Chinese porcelain makers, nodders were eventually made in the West in pottery, porcelain, bisque, wood, and even papier mâché. While only a small portion of those originally made still exist, the variety in size, style, and quality is great enough to yield continual delightful surprises to the diligent collector. Figurines of Oriental, Black, and Occidental people of all ages were made with nodding heads and hands. Both negative and positive movements were devised by careful balance of the free-floating head set on a pin that rests on the neck of each figure.

Nodders can be found that were made by some of the leading German, British, or French porcelain makers as well as some that are not easily identified today as to country of origin or factory. Few nodders are marked, but many of those found today were made in Japan, a country known for its penchant for producing inexpensive bisque novelties for the Western market. Since the Japanese porcelain manufacturers were also known to have a remarkable talent for copying any European art style, it is probable that many of the nodders *thought* to be German or English because of the style of dress or body of the pottery or porcelain used were really produced in Japan.

It doesn't really matter where a specific nodder originated: all old ones are in strong demand by collectors who relish the amusing quality of these funny little figures that come to life when touched with a finger.

NORITAKE
CHINA

Collectors who appreciate fine, hand-painted china are presently collecting all they can find that was made in Japan for export to the United States previous to World War II by the Noritake firm of Nagoya. Ceramics of high quality were imported by the import-export company of the Morimura Brothers, who established an office in New York in 1876. The decorated china was sold across this nation and was relatively inexpensive, so that almost anyone could afford it. The bulk of Noritake china collected today dates from the beginning of the century to around 1930 and represents decorative art styles ranging from Victorian to Art Nouveau and Art Deco. Many designs were "borrowed" from popular European patterns and shapes. However, most pieces have decoration that is carefully painted by artists of great talent who "married" the decoration to the shape of the fine, white porcelain. When a piece is found on which the decoration does not appear to be suitable, it is often a blank decorated in America.

The variety of shape and decoration is large in Noritake chinaware. While dinnerware constituted a large portion of the firm's export business, giftware items also were sold in quantity and these single or multiple china pieces were imaginatively made and decorated. Chocolate sets, many copied from French china sets, were very popular. Ashtrays, smoking sets, cigarette boxes, and humidors can be found. There are honey pots and figural powder boxes, dresser sets and tea sets, china swans, fish, and other animals.

Although a great many dinnerware patterns were made, collectors are especially fascinated with the "Azalea" pattern, which was once a premium item given away by a tea company. Because so many of today's generation remember the pattern as one that Grandmother used to own, this has become a nostalgia item of our time, although the quality of this giveaway china is not as high as most other Noritake patterns.

Noritake wares were marketed in an interesting manner. Sample books were made up of pages with illustrations of each piece or pattern. Pages in these books were hand-painted by the same artists who decorated the china, and shopowners or buyers would order from these books, which were carried by Morimura's salesmen. These sample books are works of art and are of special value because Noritake's business records were destroyed during the war when the company was bombed.

Collectors search for china pieces with the Noritake mark or the "M" mark of the Morimura import firm. The oldest mark, found only on pieces of very high quality, is "R.C." which stands for Royal Ceramic and dates the pieces from 1911. Many of these pieces are elaborate in design and heavily decorated and gilded.

Included in the area of Japanese collectibles are pieces marked "Nippon." These pieces date between 1891 and 1921 and are usually of a less high quality than marked Noritake. Nippon ware, however, is more often of asymmetrical design and/or decoration and its appeal to today's collector is that it is more Japanese in character.

Collecting Japanese chinaware made for the American market has been a rapidly

Pages from a Noritake salesman's hand-painted sample book show three salt-shaker designs.

growing hobby, with some collectors striving to put together complete dinner, luncheon, or tea sets in one pattern and others purchasing just the single giftware objects that were made in a large variety of shapes and decoration. Collectors who cannot afford the older, high quality Noritake or marked Morimura pieces have been buying later pieces marked "Japan" or "Made in Japan." While this ware was made after 1921, some of it is decorative and handsome.

Noritake, Nippon, or even Made in Japan items dating to the early 1940s are all in demand today. Collectors realize that most patterns and shapes will never be reproduced in the same quality with decoration by talented artists. For the lover of fine china, this is a relatively inexpensive hobby and one in which any investment today is certain to appreciate.

BOOKS:

Japanese Ceramics of the Last 100 Years, Irene Stitt. Crown Publishers, Inc., One Park Avenue, New York, New York 10016.

Sample-book page for Noritake lists shapes and sizes for plates.

Painting of a plate that appeared in the Noritake sample books. The same artists who decorated the plates painted the sample-book pages as exact replicas.

OCCULT
COLLECTIBLES

Tarot cards are a specialty within the broader area of occult collectibles.

The possibilities for collecting occult objects might run the alphabetical gamut from amulets to Zuni prayer sticks. Anything having to do with the supernatural, especially primitive objects made by hand for the practice of alchemy, magic, necromancy, or astrology, are in demand by collectors who are not afraid to gather objects that lead them into the study of the unknown.

Many collectors of the occult specialize in only one aspect of it. For instance, the practice of witchcraft might spur the imagination of one collector, while another will specialize in symbols of a fraternity such as the Masons. Occult collections include

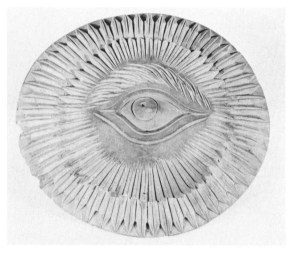

The "evil eye" is a motif often found in folk carvings of various countries.

Crystal balls and other fortune-telling devices are collectible items.

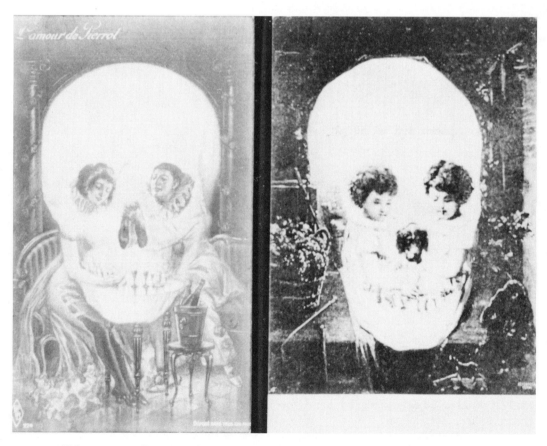

"Memento mori" postcards are collectibles made in the late nineteenth century.

tribal masks, fertility symbols, tarot cards, figures of Hindu gods, jewelry, prints, paintings, wood carvings, stone carvings, textiles, games, books, or any prehistoric, historic, or modern objects, as long as the connection to the supernatural or religious can be identified. Because there is so much in the world of art that can be connected to the occult, either through former use, material, shape, or decorative aspects, there are many specialties within this eerie area of collecting.

A renewal of interest in occultism took place in the 1960s and has led to the manufacture of new products, mostly reproductions of the old, and the publication of hundreds of books on every aspect of the occult. In addition, just about anything that had been published previously about the world of the occult has been reprinted. Almost any city in this country and England can boast of at least one occult bookshop and all of the material for practicing witchcraft is available. Crystal balls, dried bats and frogs, and even human skulls and bones are easily purchased by the modern practitioners of ancient arts. High priestesses' silver chalices, bracelets, amulets, cloaks, and all sorts of symbolic objects for spell-casting can be purchased. Some of these items are still handcrafted, but modern crystal balls are more apt to be Lucite.

Collectors search for old examples of the *atheme,* or witch's dagger. These edged symbolic weapons of witchery, as well as chalices, salt containers, incense burners, candlesticks, and pentacles, have been made through the ages for the observance of supernatural rites and are all collectible items.

All symbols that represent any of the world's religions, both ancient and modern, are considered part of the huge field of occult collecting. Even for specialists in just one of the signs of the astrological chart, the possibilities for collecting are almost endless. Such a collection would include jewelry, pottery, porcelain, glass, paintings, prints, and sculpture.

Symbols reflecting the superstition of man are collected by many, and museums give these objects of folk art prime space today. An example of the occult in American folk art would be the carved figureheads from sailing ships that were meant to guide and protect seafarers.

Voodoo dolls, talismans, amulets, and all of the magical paraphernalia ever made are wanted by both collectors and believers. Collectibles of the occult are fascinating and the quest is almost endless for objects that are old, well made, and often decorative.

BOOKS:

The Encyclopedia of Tarot, Stuart R. Kaplan. U. S. Games Systems, Inc., 468 Park Avenue South, New York, New York 10016.

PAPERWEIGHTS

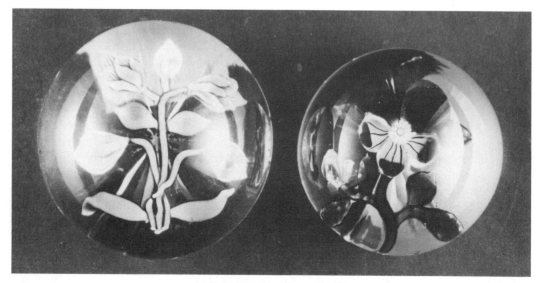

Antique Baccarat paperweights.

These small glass whimsies have been a popular collector's item since they first made their appearance in the nineteenth century. Bohemian and Venetian glassblowers preceded the French in the production of glass balls that are a tactile and visual delight. In the mid-nineteenth century French glassblowers developed the art of paperweight-making to entice users and collectors; American glassblowers came on the scene shortly after. A short decline followed in the demand for and subsequent production of blown-glass weights, until the period following World War II, when collecting the early weights led to the production of editions made expressly for collectors. This resurgence of interest pushed up the prices for the antique weights and made the introduction of new designs, as well as reproduced patterns, a profitable business for dealers all over the world. Today, the early weights as well as those made later by fine craftsmen are in high demand.

From an investment point of view, paperweights have attributes that make them extremely desirable. They are easy to store, a delight to display and admire, and, in the case of free-blown glass weights, no two are exactly alike. Most new productions are made for collectors in limited, numbered, and signed editions; many of these increase in value almost as soon as they are placed on the market.

Among the prized collectibles in the paperweight field are those made in France in the nineteenth century. Antique Baccarat weights lead the field internationally, while in the United States the small supply of weights surviving from the New England Glass Company's early production (around 1850) has made prices for these rarities soar. Contemporary paperweights, signed by the artist-glassblower who designed and made them, are priced according to the uniqueness of the colors and patterns as well as the reputation of the glassblower.

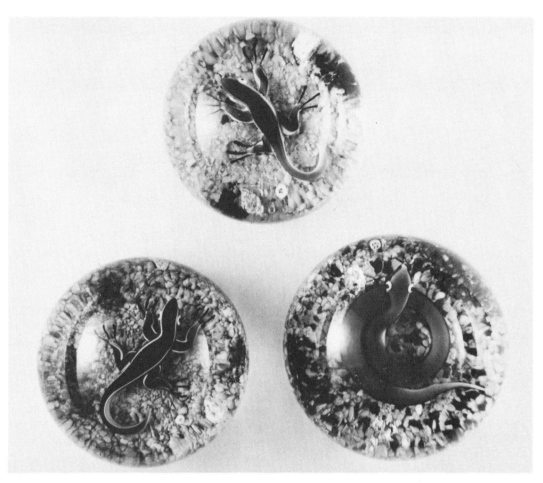

Modern Baccarat paperweights are made in limited editions and are "instant" collector's items.

Antique paperweights made by St. Louis (left) and Clichy.

Modern portrait sulphide paperweights of Will Rogers and Theodore Roosevelt were made by Baccarat.

Careful study and purchasing of modern glass paperweights can lead to the building of a unique and valuable collection for a moderate investment. A source for these would be attendance at regional crafts shows and exhibits. Visits to galleries where the work of contemporary glassblowers is shown may also lead to successful purchases.

A comprehensive collection of paperweights should include some of the old along with the new series that are issued by leading glassmakers. The more complicated the design encased in glass, the more apt the weight is to increase in value. The glassblower can show off his sense of color and pattern in the medium of the paperweight without having to concern himself with the utilitarian value of the object. Like most glass whimsies, the paperweight is often made just for the pleasure of turning out a blob of colorful glass arranged in a pleasing pattern.

When you are considering the purchase of new weights, the reputation of the glassblower is of primary importance. Established glassblowers whose outputs are limited are outdoing each other in producing small numbers of glorious weights. Some market their limited editions only through established dealers of paperweights. These dealers have lists of collectors willing to invest in each new issue produced by well-known artists. Companies such as Baccarat and D'Albret also offer partial or complete editions of designs to these few specialist dealers.

As an investment, paperweights historically are among the top collectibles. A new paperweight can often be purchased for a few dollars, but the top price recently paid for a rare weight is $21,000. Collecting in this category requires a knowledge of how glass is made, an awareness of which glassblowers are presently producing weights in limited editions, and some discretion in purchasing advertised "limited editions" that are produced in large quantities. Be certain you know how "limited" an edition really is, since some companies limit the amounts they produce of a certain design by the amount they are able to produce and sell within a certain period of time. In the case of artist-made and -signed editions, there are few glassblowers who can produce an appreciable number of one type of paperweight without becoming bored. There are some truly outstanding glassblowers working in several countries today, and their contemporary work is well worth owning.

CLUBS:

American Paperweight Guild
P. O. Box 177
Atlantic City, New Jersey 08404

BOOKS:

Antique and Contemporary Paperweights, An Illustrated Catalog and Price Guide, L. H. Selman. Order from author, L. H. Selman Ltd., 761 Chestnut Street, Santa Cruz, California 95060.

The Encyclopedia of Glass Paperweights, Paul Hollister. Clarkson N. Potter, Inc., 419 Park Avenue South, New York, New York 10016.

Paperweights for Collectors, Lawrence H. Selman and Linda Pope-Selman. Paperweight Press, Box 400, Santa Cruz, California 95060.

PHOTOGRAPHIC IMAGES

Sixth-plate daguerreotype by Southworth and Hawes of Boston would be a prized item for any image collector.

Anyone who had the foresight to collect photographic images only a few years ago has watched his or her investment grow in great proportion to the original investment. Not too many years ago, daguerreotypes, ambrotypes, tintypes, stereo views, and other nineteenth-century images lay neglected in attics, drawers, and old trunks, and one could buy a box lot of this material at auction for a few dollars. Frequently, the buyer would remove the image and use the old, decorative frames for display of more recent family photographs.

Vintage images of national figures have spiraled in price so much that the discovery of an unknown picture of Lincoln or any other nineteenth-century American hero is cause for news releases. Any new discovery of the work of American photographer Mathew Brady is also a matter of great interest to the historian-collectors.

For the purists in image-collecting, the daguerreotypes are the most wanted of all old images, since these are one-of-a-kind photographs and the process used was the first that was commercially successful. Among the most desirable of all early photographers' work is that of the firm of Southworth and Hawes of Boston, Massachusetts, and one well-known collector has amassed images and equipment purchased from heirs of one of these partners. This astute collector's display includes not only some of the finest daguerreotype images, distinguished by the strength and artistic arrangement of the poses and by the clarity and grace of the pictures, but also handwritten records of the partnership and other related objects such as posing chairs from their studio.

Other sought-after specialties in daguerreotypes are pictures of deceased children, all outdoor scenes, Civil War pictures, photographs of the West which include gold-mining operations in California, pictures showing any nineteenth-century occupation and occupational costumes, commercial and residential structures, and especially, any pictures having to do with the history of the art of photography. All ad-

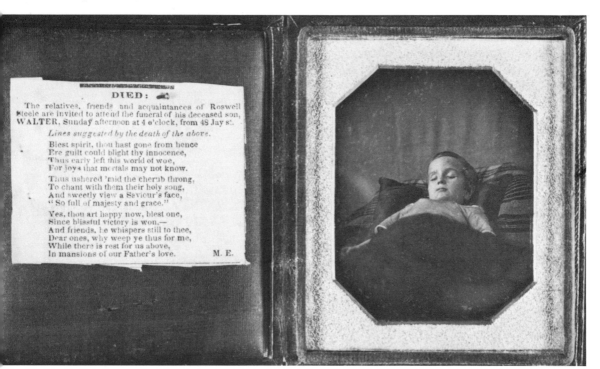

Collectors of early photographic images look for memorial photographs taken of corpses. Those of children are especially poignant.

Fine daguerreotype of American sailor by W. H. Lewis of New York City. Sixth-plate size, the image is delicately tinted.

vertising material, such as signs, trade cards, or handbills, that add to our knowledge of the history of early photography are also collected as related material. Another speciality within this highly specialized field of daguerreotype collectibles is the collecting of miniature images mounted as jewelry.

Later images, such as stereo cards that are not of the more common variety, are eagerly sought. A collector might go through boxes and boxes of these cards at an antique show, flea market, or photographic show and come up with just one or two gems. The discarded double images would include views of foreign places frequently photographed, nonphotographic views of the Grand Canyon or American Indians, or items with religious themes, which were printed by the thousands. Instead, the knowledgeable collector searches for the earlier images published by the Anthonys in New York or the Langenheim brothers of Philadelphia. All views having to do with photographic history, such as the interior of a photographer's studio or images that show any photographic equipment are of great value, both monetarily and historically.

BOOKS:

Collection, Use and Care of Historical Photographs, Robert A. Weinstein and Larry Booth. The American Association for State and Local History, 1400 Eighth Avenue South, Nashville, Tennessee 37203.

Photographica, A Guide to the Value of Historic Cameras and Images, Charles Klamkin with Matthew Isenberg. Funk & Wagnalls, 10 East 53rd Street, New York, New York 10022.

PHOTOGRAPHICA, THE EQUIPMENT

George Eastman's original Kodak camera, introduced in 1888, once sold for $25. With box and carrying case, this outfit is worth $5,000 today.

Those dealers and collectors knowledgeable and astute enough to have begun amassing the collectibles of photography as recently as five years ago have seen their collections increase in value beyond just about any other investment they could have made. Collecting cameras and old photographic equipment, as well as printed matter having to do with the history of photography, is a recent hobby that has captured the interest of hundreds of enthusiasts, but there are few examples of old and rare items on the market. This has made prices rise quickly for the documented nineteenth-century

Kodaks, once owned by many American families, are valuable collector's items now. Shown are models in the "A," "B," and "C" series made in 1891.

items. As more and more people become enthralled with this collecting specialty, the prices for the real rarities have risen so fast that a price guide is obsolete before it can be put into print.

Areas of specialization in the field of photographica are prephotographic, Daguerreian, and wet-plate equipment, classic European cameras, cameras and related material made by George Eastman and the Eastman Kodak Company, detective cameras, miniature cameras, spy cameras, early color cameras and equipment, Leicas, early 35-mm cameras, single- and twin-reflex cameras, and twentieth-century stereo and special-purpose cameras. All accessories and printed matter pertaining to these areas of specialization and illustrating the history of the development of photography are in high demand.

The collectibles of photography form the basis of a worldwide hobby and it is not unusual for the more affluent dealers and collectors to place bids at any auction in the world where a rare camera is being sold. Specialist collectors know every model made within their areas of interest and each variation of those models—and they want them all. When one is dealing with a type of camera such as the Leica, where changes in production and accessories have resulted in enormous numbers of cameras and equip-

ment with subtle refinements, this can be a lifetime quest and represent a huge investment for anyone new to the field of Leica collecting.

The most expensive and most esoteric way in which to specialize in photographica is to collect only the cameras, equipment, and ephemera associated with the birth and infancy of photography, roughly the period between 1839 and 1865. This type of specialized collecting, available now only to the very affluent, would include daguerreian cameras, their stands, plates, preparation and developing apparatus, and the same type of materials used in wet-plate photography. Since most of the prime materials of this era are in museums or in a few spectacular private collections, there is little documented material or equipment from this early period that comes on the market. When it does, competition for it is fierce.

BOOKS:

Antique Cameras, R. C. Smith. David and Charles Company, Ltd., North Pomfret, Vermont 05053.

Photographica, A Guide to the Value of Historic Cameras and Images, Charles Klamkin with Matthew Isenberg. Funk & Wagnalls, 10 East 53rd Street, New York, New York 10022.

PICTURE POSTCARDS

Buster Brown advertising postcards by R. F. Outceault. One advertises shoes while the other is a Christmas advertisement for Bloomingdale's department store.

They're called "deltiologists" and if you don't think the collecting of picture postcards can be a science, *you* try sorting out and listing according to subject, artist, and publisher the hundreds of thousands of picture postcards that were published during the heyday of the art, 1880 to 1918. The range of subjects and categories is vast, but most postcards fit into one of three major categories: view cards, comics, and greetings. However, a collector can specialize in a single subject such as transportation or disasters or Thanksgiving greetings and still amass collections that will number in the thousands.

Since they were originally published *for* collectors, picture postcards are a natural hobby for those interested in geography, history, politics, art, photography, costume, disasters, or hundreds of other special subjects. Before the turn of the century the world was inundated with picture postcards.

They were collected in fancy albums and used to cover lampshades, screens, and wastebaskets. Many cards were produced in series and sets and the picture postcard also became the medium on which manufacturers and retailers could advertise their wares for very little investment. There were funny cards: some, depicting Blacks, mothers-in-law, women, and henpecked husbands, do not seem as funny today as they may have seemed in the last century. There were cards made for every special occasion, every holiday, and to appeal to people of every age and personality. Not a city or town existed that didn't have its Main Street recorded for posterity on picture postcards sold at the local drugstore.

Postcards were embossed, die-cut, and sometimes had added material such as feathers, fabric, or real hair. For the children, there were paper doll cards, puzzle cards, and "installment" cards, mailed on

New Year's greeting postcards.

four successive days until all four received made up a single picture and poem. The variety of collectible picture postcards is enormous and represents a rather complete picture of the Edwardian era.

Picture postcards are collected today according to their rarity, subject matter, and various other criteria that are sometimes regional in nature. A few years ago this was an inexpensive hobby, with many collectors spending time and effort to list all available cards in their major fields of interest. These published lists, which made it easier for new collectors with similar interests to identify their purchases, spread the excitement of the revival of postcard collecting. Added to this was the recognition of the picture postcard as a form of popular art by museums

and colleges, and several major exhibits opened with great media fanfare.

The result of this widespread revival of picture postcard collecting as a hobby is the formation of new clubs, publication of new lists of special subjects, and a rapid rise in prices. Nevertheless, the number of available postcards is so vast that there are still many areas of specialization open to new collectors who do not want to invest heavily in their hobby. In addition, a great deal of trading goes on. (You can probably get two "kittens" for one "courthouse," but railroad depots are another story.)

LINCOLN'S ADDRESS AT GETTYSBURG.

Some collectors specialize in picture postcards showing Abraham Lincoln. There are hundreds.

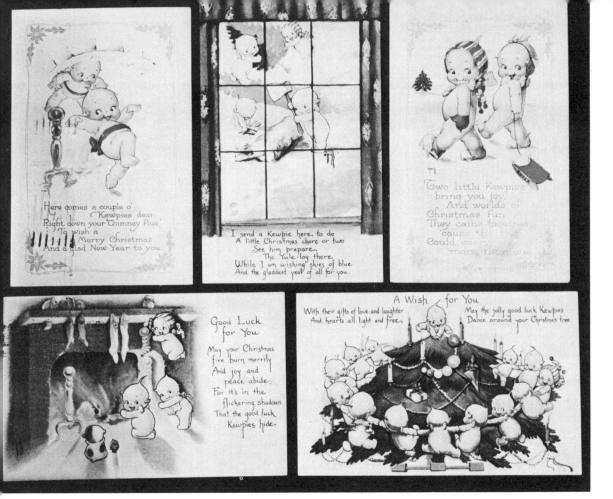

Rose O'Neill's Kewpies were favorite subjects for postcards when they were new and are sought by today's collector.

BOOKS:

Picture Postcards, Marian Klamkin. Dodd, Mead & Company, 79 Madison Avenue, New York, New York 10016.

Picture Postcards in the United States, 1893–1918, George and Dorothy Miller. Clarkson N. Potter, Inc., 419 Park Avenue South, New York, New York 10016.

CLUBS:

Deltiologists of America
James L. Lowe
3709 Gradyville Road
Newton Square, Pennsylvania 19073

Metropolitan Postcard Collectors Club
Irving Dolin
140 East 8th Street
New York, New York 10013

International Post Card Collectors
    Association
W. Von Boltenstern
6380 Wilshire Boulevard, Suite 907
Los Angeles, California 90048

The Nostalgiana Collectors Club
Allen Wright
440 West 34th Street, Apt. 1-A
New York, New York 10001

Postcard Club Federation
John McClintock
Box 27
Somerdale, New Jersey 08083

Sunbonnet baby series shows subjects that were used as decoration on other objects, such as children's feeding plates and mugs.

Anthropomorphic cats by Louis Wain were popular postcard subjects during the golden era of postcard production.

POLITICAL CAMPAIGN ITEMS

To attend a show of political campaign items is to be present at a panorama of years of pageant, promises, and platitudes. The losers and the winners are all represented by badges and buttons, banners, posters, stickers, plates, mugs, bandannas, banks, matchbooks, paperweights, and hundreds of other items that were given away or sold. All represent the history of American politics.

By far the largest group of political item collectors are those who specialize in campaign buttons. Most of these collectors specialize in presidential buttons, candidates of home states only, or the buttons of one candidate or election. Some specialize in congressional elections or search only for the buttons that have become scarce and valuable. For instance, the buttons that represent the 1920 campaign of James M. Cox and his running mate, Franklin Delano Roosevelt, are prime items among political button collectors. The winners in that election, Warren Harding and Calvin Coolidge, are also represented on buttons that bring high prices today. In determining the value of campaign buttons, it isn't who won or lost, but the number of buttons that are available, and in that election, there weren't a lot of buttons issued.

Celluloid buttons are generally more valuable than lithographed buttons. "Jugates," buttons with pictures of two candidates together, are desirable items. Not all buttons were given away. Some were sold to raise campaign funds and these larger and more elaborate buttons are usually more expensive.

Buttons for presidential candidates and running mates are desirable and collectible.

Public admiration for a candidate of the past is sometimes a criterion for scarcity and high prices. There are so many Kennedy admirers that buttons for both John's and Robert's campaigns are in demand. On the other hand, Nixon buttons are wanted by Watergate collectors. At present, there is a strong demand for buttons of women who have run for political office, women's suffrage buttons, or ERA buttons.

Political item collectors are historians who save all the ephemeral items that represent the country's political past. Sheet

Thomas A. Hendricks, now a forgotten name, was Grover Cleveland's running mate in the presidential election of 1884. Hendricks died in 1885. This plate was a campaign item.

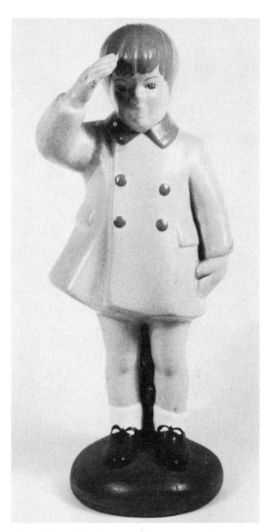

Not all political items are in good taste. This ceramic figure shows John Kennedy's son saluting at his father's funeral.

Glass paperweight for a candidate from Elwood, Indiana.

Campaign ashtray made for the late Senator Everett McKinley Dirksen.

Toby mug of Theodore Roosevelt in his "Rough Rider" garb is a memento of his term as President.

One of few Watergate items, this poster was designed as an in-house joke by an advertising agency.

Political campaign cup.

music, picture postcards, pencils, pens, dinner invitations, and menus for campaign or victory banquets are bought or traded among these collectors. The buttons are a large part of political collectors' lives, but the less available items are always welcome additions to collections.

CLUBS:

American Political Items Collectors
66 Golf Street
Newington, Connecticut 06111

BOOKS:

Encyclopedia of Political Buttons, United States, 1896–1972, Ted Hake. Joy Products, 24 West 45th Street, New York, New York 10036.

The Illustrated Political Button Book. California Political Items Company, P. O. Box 1741J, Santa Cruz, California 95060.

Political Buttons, Book II 1920–1976, Ted Hake. Hake's Americana and Collectibles Press, P. O. Box 1444, York, Pennsylvania 17405.

PRIVATE MINT COLLECTIBLES

There are thousands of people who invested in "limited edition" collectibles made by the Franklin Mint, the Danbury Mint, and other companies with "official" sounding names in the hope that their manufactured new items would soon go up in value. At its height, for instance, the Franklin Mint issued as many as 150 programs for the collector. Persuasive direct mail pieces promised everything but a written guarantee that the secondary market in their ingots, plaques, plates, coins, books, medallions, sculpture, and other items would bring profits greater than investment in stock or other more conventional commodities.

For a while, what *did* go up considerably in value was Franklin Mint stock. *Forbes* magazine, as early as August 1, 1976, stated that the Franklin Mint managed to produce "collectibles for middle-class tastes and pocketbooks—and it turns out to be almost incredibly profitable." Within nine years an investment in Franklin Mint stock had appreciated 6,800%.

There were thousands of collectors who invested in series with titles such as "Fifty State Bicentennial," "First Ladies," "History of Flight," "Signers of the Declaration." As series were completed, those wishing to dispose of their collections for hard cash were usually dismayed to find out that it was impossible to recoup their investment —or, in many cases, to find any buyers at all. The only intrinsic value, they found out, was in the metal.

Collectors' magazines, often hard up for the regular advertising that helps support them, appeared to add to the excitement of the new collector's items: first, by accepting many full-page advertisements, and second, by touting new "artistic" issues in articles. This kind of editorial support gave skeptical collectors confidence that they were investing in ready-made collectibles that would, indeed, escalate in value as inflation continued and the value of the dollar dropped.

In November, 1978, the television show "60 Minutes" interviewed collectors who had become disenchanted with their investment in Franklin Mint collector's items. Also interviewed in the segment were dealers who were realistic about the resale value of Franklin Mint items, especially those made of precious metals such as silver or gold. The viewer was left with the impression, undoubtedly real, that the collectibles were only worth their value as molten metal, certainly a lower value than was paid for them originally. The television show told those who know the collecting market nothing they did not already know. Many of the series made by Franklin Mint were issued in quantities ranging from 10,000 to 100,000. These could hardly be called "rare, limited editions" and it was obvious that if there were to be a profitable secondary market, many generations would have to pass.

Following the CBS show, Charles Andes, Franklin Mint chairman, refuted "60 Minutes," labeling the show "false," and blamed the program for causing Franklin Mint stock to drop. He claimed that CBS attempted to discredit Franklin Mint in order to push its own direct mail Columbia House business.

For some investors in Franklin Mint and other manufacturers' collectibles, things have changed since 1978. Those items made of sterling silver are becoming worth their original buying price simply because the price of silver has risen sharply. Most Franklin Mint items are never going to be worth their original price, but those made of heavy silver do finally have a respectable market. Value is set according to the going price of silver and the weight of the ingots, coins, or other Franklin Mint objects. Collectors aren't interested in them, but the metal smelters are.

There is a danger in purchasing any newly manufactured collector's items as investment. The appeal for Americans is that there is no knowledge necessary to purchase by mail order any series of plates, coins, ingots, medallions, thimbles, or many other of the "instant collectibles" offered to you if you are on the right computerized mailing lists. To purchase plates from the Bradford Exchange or coins from the Franklin Mint with the idea that you are buying something that will go up in value is foolhardy. The only reason to buy any of these collectibles is that you like them, enjoy displaying them, and believe them to have some artistic merit. Manufacturers of new collector's items continue to bombard the mails with new offers. Even a television program with the clout of "60 Minutes" cannot completely discourage this typically American habit of writing a check to any company that starts a direct mail piece with the words, "Dear Friend."

RAILROADIANA

Old railway calendars are hard to come by and very desirable.

Collectibles related to the development of railroading in America cover a wide range of items that together depict the history and rapid expansion of nineteenth-century America. There are very few collecting pursuits that can boast of so many dedicated and enthusiastic buffs as railroadiana. The collecting of timetables, tickets, sheet music, postcards, dining car ceramics and silver, badges, lanterns, locks and keys, stock certificates from long-defunct railroads, uniform items, and hundreds of other pieces of memorabilia has grown very rapidly within the past decade.

Advertising items, many printed in lavish color and die-cut in wonderful patterns, represent the heyday of railroad travel, from the early times of the narrow-gauge Colorado railroads built to service mining camps to the streamliners of this century. All paper memorabilia—including calendars printed as giveaways by many rail lines, as well as beautifully engraved stock certificates—are in great demand and are carefully documented and preserved by railroadiana collectors.

The more obscure the defunct railroad lines represented by a collectible item, the

Timetables are probably the most desired of all railroad-connected items.

more valuable that item is apt to become. Some collectors specialize in only the memorabilia of a single train or rail line, while others branch out to collect one type of item from all lines. There are collectors who only buy dining car dishes or silver, while others purchase picture postcards showing the great number of train stations built in this country during the peak period of railroad travel. Since many of these de-

pots, built in a variety of architectural styles, have been torn down, often a picture postcard is the only record of the buildings having existed. Dining car menus, sometimes listing meals consisting of eight or ten courses, are another major collectible area. Handsomely printed annual passes, issued to employees of the railroads, are yet another specialty.

Railroadiana fans are always strong his-

OCTOBER, 1885.   FOLDER D.

St·Paul·Minneapolis & Manitoba·R'y

RED RIVER VALLEY LINE   RED RIVER VALLEY LINE

S.P.M.&M.R'y
Double Track Stone Arch Bridge
Minneapolis, Minn.

Through the Park Region to the New Northwest

W. S. ALEXANDER,   C. H. WARREN,   JAS. J. HILL,   A. MANVEL,
General Traffic Manager,   General Passenger Agent,   President,   General Manager,
ST. PAUL, MINN.   ST. PAUL, MINN.

Timetable printed in 1885.

tory buffs. Within their specialty one can find printed material enticing people from various European countries to settle the wilderness of America opened up by the building of railroads. "Homes for the homeless" was one phrase used to attract settlers. For those interested in labor union memorabilia, there are many items connected with railroads from which to choose. This category might include badges, awards, pins, buttons, posters, handbills, and other reminders of the railroad workers' struggle for fair treatment. This material dates from the decade following the Civil War and the printed material, especially, depicts both sides of the battle.

Old depot signs, train signs, and posters that once covered the walls of the depots and provided reading matter for waiting passengers are all desirable collector's

Tickets, passes, and other paper railroadiana items are treasured by railroad buffs.

items. Another major area of specialization is railroad mail memorabilia. Trains had their own post offices in separate cars, and cancelled stamps on mail that was handled by these long-defunct traveling post offices depict interesting postal history.

Related fields of interest for the railroad enthusiast are trolley car memorabilia and toy train sets.

BOOKS:

The Collector's Book of Railroadiana, Stanley L. Baker and Virginia Brainard Kunz. Hawthorn/Dutton, 2 Park Avenue, New York, New York 10016.

Railroad Collectibles, A Price Guide, Howard Johnson. L-W Promotions, Box 69, Gas City, Indiana 46933.

Railroadiana, A Collector's Guide to Railroad Memorabilia, Charles Klamkin. Funk & Wagnalls, 10 East 53rd Street, New York, New York 10022.

CLUBS:

National Association of Timetable
 Collectors
Fred Carnes
185 South Highland Avenue
Ossining, New York 10562

Railway advertising fan was a necessary giveaway before air-conditioned cars.

Dining car china, such as this popular Pullman pattern, are much-sought-after railroadiana items.

Uniform buttons, badges, caps, and even uniforms are collector's items.

RUSSIAN
LACQUER BOXES

Russian lacquer box, made before Revolution, shows young woman coming out a door to meet her lover, who is hidden in the bushes.

Hardly anyone today can afford to collect Fabergé boxes and other silver or gold jewel-studded trinkets of the Czars. There are other Russian boxes that have had less attention from writers on collectibles, but are certainly being collected in some quantity and are, by many, equally revered for their workmanship and beauty. These boxes are the work of talented artists and craftspeople who have managed to continue an ancient Russian art form throughout this century. While the lacquer boxes and other objects made and decorated with the same techniques as those used by ancient icon makers are expensive, there are still some bargains to be found.

Russian lacquer boxes that are being made today have two types of decoration; those painted in fanciful scenes derived from Russian folk tales, and others with genre scenes that are either contemporary or historical in style. Both are handsome

The troika is a motif used often in Russian art. This old lacquer box is undated, but is probably late nineteenth century.

Hand-painted lid of pre-Revolutionary Russian lacquer box shows a couple at a gate.

and highly desirable, but most present-day collectors prefer the painted scenes depicting Russian people in everyday life. The boxes, made in the village of Palekh, are produced for export in small amounts by artists who sign each tiny painted box cover. To make collecting Russian lacquer boxes a fairly simple matter, traditionally each box has been dated. Certain artists' work is considered of masterpiece quality, and all collectors have their favorites among both older and contemporary work.

The methods used to make and decorate the papier mâché lacquered boxes have been handed down from generation to generation in the small town of Palekh. For-

mulas for the hard black or red lacquer have been carefully guarded. The paintings are directly applied to the lids by artists who pride themselves on their ability to work in miniature, often working with a magnifying glass, and the colorful, detailed paintings are magnificent works of art.

Contemporary Russian lacquer boxes can be found from time to time in fine gift or jewelry stores. Unless one is a collector or has knowledge of how Palekh boxes are made and decorated, prices seem high for the new boxes. Knowledgeable people realize that each box lid is an example of a fine, original miniature painting and an art form that was almost lost to the world.

Because Russian lacquer is not well known in the West, and there has only recently been a reawakening in Russia concerning the continuance of folk art forms, there occasionally is a good buy in today's antiques market for the older lacquer boxes. Some of these are priced more reasonably due to dealers' lack of knowledge concerning the techniques used in making the boxes or the artistry involved.

If one's taste is for more primitive types of Russian art, there are hand-carved and -painted peasant-style boxes that were made at the beginning of this century. These can sometimes be found in house sales or auctions and usually are not priced very high.

Two small boxes (left) 1941; (right) 1965.

Handsomely painted large lacquer box shows young woman in peasant dress with Russian towers in the background. The box is dated 1955.

They are colorful and handsome and will become more valuable with time. Another kind of Russian box to look for is the pressed glass jewelry box made in the nineteenth century. These are usually made of clear glass with metal hinges and trim, but there are some in colored glass. All forms of pre-Revolutionary Russian art are worth collecting, but the three types of small boxes mentioned above have special appeal for today's collector.

BOOKS:

The Collector's Book of Boxes, Marian Klamkin. Dodd, Mead & Company, 79 Madison Avenue, New York, New York 10016.

SCHOOLHOUSE COLLECTIBLES

Self-explanatory picture postcard.

In this era of electronic teaching devices and audiovisual material that turns teachers and students into passive observers and by-standers, the objects of the old one-room schoolhouse have taken on more meaning than ever. A term often used by today's educators is "hands-on materials," by which they mean teaching materials that the student actually holds while he or she is learning. Students of the one-room schoolhouse had only "hands-on" materials, and collectors now search for all of the items once held and used by teachers and students. These include early textbooks such as the McGuffey reader, hornbooks, slates, book carriers, and all appurtenances of the early classroom. Pencil boxes, slate erasers, crayons and crayon boxes, and chalk are also desirable. Lunch boxes, ranging from wooden buckets to store-bought metal containers, are part of this collecting category and some schoolhouse collectors look for more modern lunch boxes that have illustrations of cartoon characters or television characters that were popular in the 1950s.

Master ink bottles made of pottery were often seen around the classroom in the last century.

Teachers' handbells made of brass or bell metal with turned wooden handles have been collector's items for a long time, but a more recent, and perhaps more authentic schoolhouse bell being collected today is the desk-type tap bell. All bells are difficult to find and those that can be identified as having been used in the classroom are especially elusive.

Old school desks, abundant during the

Rewards of Merit were presented to students as encouragement.

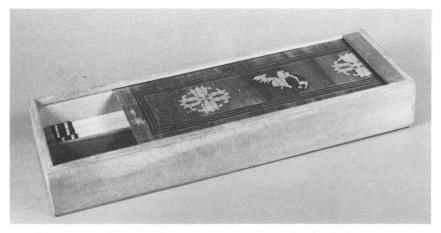

Pencil box with a sliding tambour top was made in Japan for American students.

school-building boom of the 1960s, are now becoming scarce and expensive. Within two decades, these metal-based, wood-topped desks with holes for inkwells have passed from the realm of unwanted used furniture to valued relics of the past. Other items valued by collectors are teachers' desks and chairs, pointers, schoolroom maps and charts, and rewards or certificates of merit. Early printed material associated with public education such as diplomas, graduation certificates, and programs are also collector's items.

Steel-nibbed pens and the elusive inkwells that fit into the desk-hole are schoolhouse items that are often hard to find. Most collectors also want at least one or two master ink bottles made of pottery or glass. Sharpeners for pencils or for slate markers from the last century or the early decades of this century are collected. These include small, individual sharpeners as well as the one that used to be attached to the teacher's desk. Erasers, paints, brushes, and kindergarten toys are ephemeral items that help complete this special area of collecting.

SHEET MUSIC

Sheet music has been published throughout America's history to record every accomplishment from "aeronaut" to astronaut.

It's more than just musical history. The old sheet music of our nation covers all aspects of life through two centuries, it's true. However, the collectors of old sheet music look for cover art as well as musical or lyrical contents. The covers are a history of popular art and as such are in great demand by many who have only recently discovered that they can still find covers engraved by Nathaniel Currier, Endicott of Boston, or Bufford of New York, literally for a song.

For those more interested in history than art, there are many specializations within the huge collecting area of American sheet music. Transportation development, including anything from bicycles to railroads to airplanes, dirigibles, and balloons to sailing ships and steamships to automobiles, is one huge specialty. One might specialize in political sheet music, narrow one's interest even further to campaign songs, and still amass a huge collection.

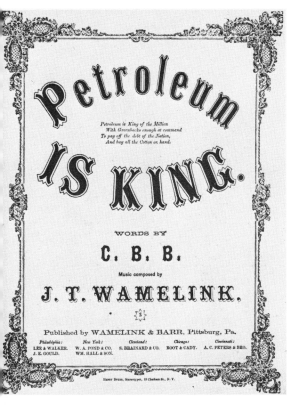

Prophetic song title written a century ago. Another "song for the times" that is still pertinent.

The history of the development of dance is another aspect of sheet music collecting and there are thousands of devotees of the American musical theater or musical films who delight in collecting all of the original sheet music published for these special interests.

Social causes such as temperance, women's rights, wars, and Black history have appeal to many collectors, while others purchase songs with a single theme such as mothers or home. There are at least a hundred ways one can direct the search for old sheet music. Often, sheet music will become an important aspect of a celebrity collection. For example, collectors of Shirley Temple items may want all sheet music having the child star's picture on the cover.

From an artistic aspect, old sheet music carries one through the history of engraving and lithography to early photography and color printing. Big Band collectors search for the sheet music of the Thirties and Forties that feature youthful photographs of the band leaders and performers of those decades and anything else that tells them something of the history of the golden age of radio.

There have been only a few real collectors of old sheet music in past decades who realized the wealth of information and art to be found in the popular music published throughout our history. These few cataloged much of what they collected; some gave their collections to libraries where they could be studied. Within the past decade, thousands of new collectors have discovered old sheet music as an enjoyable, instructive, and rewarding hobby that is still not prohibitively expensive and in which there are still many delightful surprises to be found. As stereos have taken the place of the old family upright, the sheet music industry as we once knew it has become all but obsolete. Of the many millions of pieces of sheet music published in the past, only knowledgeable collectors are preserving what is most important.

BOOKS:

Old Sheet Music, A Pictorial History, Marian Klamkin. Hawthorn Books, Inc., 260 Madison Avenue, New York, New York 10016.

Picture the Songs, Lithographs from the Sheet Music of Nineteenth-Century America, Lester S. Levy. The Johns Hopkins University Press, Baltimore, Maryland 21218.

Singer Kate Smith on the cover of a World War II song.

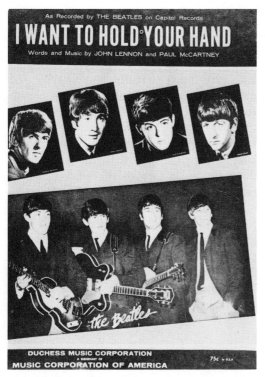

This sheet music is a popular item for collectors of "Beatlemania."

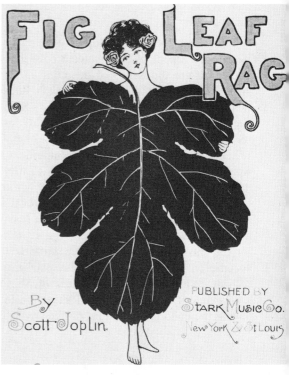

Handsome sheet music cover for one of Scott Joplin's hit ragtime tunes.

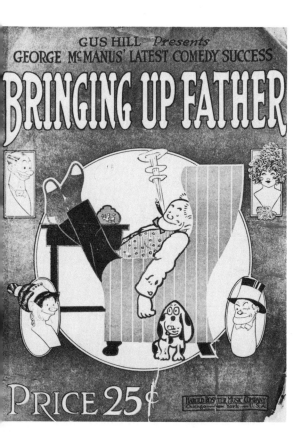

Above left, music has been written for every presidential candidate.

Above right, handsomely engraved nineteenth-century sheet music is the most desirable type in this collecting category. This music, honoring Fanny Elssler on her American tour, is especially important.

Left, sheet music cover of interest to comic collectors who are acquainted with Maggie and Jiggs. Published in 1914.

SHIRLEY TEMPLE COLLECTIBLES

When the Oscars were awarded in 1934, Shirley Temple, then six years old and the major star of Darryl F. Zanuck's Twentieth Century studio, was presented a miniature Oscar for bringing "more happiness to millions of children and millions of adults than any child of her years in the history of the world." She had already appeared in eight films and starred in half of them.

Those people who were children during the Thirties—especially those who saw all of the Temple films and remember them as wonderful escapist entertainment during the Depression years—do not question the growing numbers of collectors who seek out any of the relics that record the Temple films, her life, or the hundreds of products endorsed by the child star. The Shirley Temple dolls, watches, coloring books, movie stills, posters, mugs, cereal bowls, and hundreds of other Temple-related objects of the Thirties are actively bought, collected, traded, and sold.

Sheet music of Shirley's best-known film songs, such as "On the Good Ship Lollipop," "Baby Take a Bow," "Animal Crackers in My Soup," or "That's What I Want for Christmas," all with Shirley's photograph on the covers, have begun to zoom in price. Picture postcards advertising the Temple films and even ads cut from old magazines that show the diminutive star endorsing products about which she could have known nothing are now in strong demand by collectors. Any movie fan magazines of the period with articles or photos of the star are also considered rare items.

The most desirable Temple items, however, are the dolls made in a variety of sizes and the almost limitless wardrobes that were sold along with them. Accompanying paraphernalia are doll carriages, wardrobe trunks, doll dishes, and hundreds of other toys.

As collectible Americana, Shirley Temple items represent for many a type of optimism and innocence that the country needed in the mid-Thirties, as well as a role-model success story that influenced the lives of many of those who were children during the Depression. In the eyes of the admirers and collectors who search for every available Temple item, the child star was frozen in time on the silver screen. Their collections of books, toys, and other Temple items are proof that the dimpled, curly-haired Hollywood goldmine can remain, in their memories, just as she was when she became the idol of millions of Americans.

BOOKS:

Shirley Temple Dolls and Collectibles, P. R. Smith. Crown Publishers, One Park Avenue, New York, New York 10016.

The Shirley Temple Treasury. Random House, 201 East 50th Street, New York, New York 10022.

The World and Shirley Temple, May Neumann. McGrain Publications, Inc., P. O. Box 219-E, Frederick, Maryland 21701.

Shirley Temple paper doll and her paper doll. As if that were not enough, there was a Shirley Temple paper doll "over two feet tall."

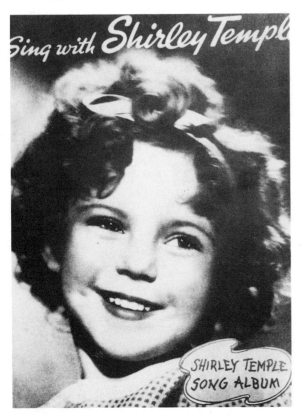

Shirley Temple Song Album *and* Shirley Temple coloring book.

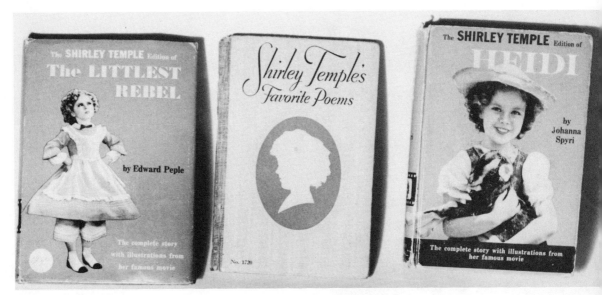

Three of the many Shirley Temple books for yesterday's children and today's adult collectors.

Shirley Temple pitcher. There were several versions of this blue glass breakfast set. Pieces were given away with food products.

Above and left, Shirley Temple dolls were made in a great variety of sizes with costumes from all of her movies.

Above and on opposite page, sheet music from films featuring the child star was a sure seller. Adult actors always got second or third billing.

SILVER

Collecting silver can be a satisfying and profitable hobby. For the person who believes in hedging all bets, silver is historically a metal that increases in value when inflation hits. The recent price rise of new silver flatware is an indication that a collection of old silver—especially those pieces marked by artists of the past whose work has always been in demand—will keep going up as more and more collectors search for safe investments in antiques and collectibles.

The obvious best investment in silver is that made during the Georgian period (eighteenth and early nineteenth centuries), but these pieces are now scarce. The new collector usually settles for later pieces of marked English or American silver. Art Nouveau, Art Deco, and early twentieth-century silver is now considered prime collecting material. Marked Tiffany, silver designed by Georg Jensen, and Russian silver of the pre-Revolution period are all desirable areas in which a new collector might specialize with the knowledge that his or her investment is a safe one.

Another method of specialization is to limit one's collection to one type of item, such as silver match safes, cigarette boxes of the early twentieth century, or even spoons of one silversmith. Wine tasters have become another popular specialty among silver collectors.

The new collector must learn the hallmarks, how to recognize patterns, what silver is the most desirable from the collector's and investor's point of view, and relative prices on today's market. There are still opportunities in this field for the neophyte as long as he or she is willing to take time to read the many excellent books on the subject.

Pair of French serving spoons with figures of Marie Antoinette and Louis XVI.

BOOKS:

Encyclopedia of American Silver Manufacturers, Dorothy T. Rainwater. Crown Publishers, Inc., One Park Avenue, New York, New York 10016.

Official Guide to Silver-Silverplate and Their Makers, 1865–1920, Carl F. Lucky. House of Collectibles, 771 Kirkman Road, Suite 100, Orlando, Florida 32811.

Tiffany Silver, Charles H. Carpenter, Jr., with Mary Grace Carpenter. Dodd, Mead & Company, 79 Madison Avenue, New York, New York 10016.

Silver-backed Art Nouveau mirror. Many dresser sets were made in this style.

Sterling silver compote made by Georg Jensen at the beginning of this century.

Sterling silver cocktail shaker made by Georg Jensen around 1930.

SOAPSTONE CARVINGS

Soapstone carvings were popular at the beginning of this century and are once again being collected. Vase and bookends.

It was called "the poor man's jade," but was soft enough to be intricately carved by Asian artists into three-dimensional openwork patterns. Small decorative objects made of steatite or soapstone were extremely popular as gift items in the first two decades of this century, when the desire for anything Japanese or Chinese was strong. This chameleon material, either in its natural colors ranging from gray to black or dyed to resemble the various soft shades of jade, was carved into vases, bookends, toothpick holders, small jars, trays, and coasters.

Most of the Chinese and Japanese soapstone carvings are undercut designs of vines, leaves, flowering plants, and trees. There are also some delightful figural carvings. Collectors today search for any of the old soapstone carvings they can find that are still in good condition. Because of the softness of the material, these small carvings were easily broken; of the many once imported, few have survived intact.

The new collector can easily tell soapstone from the materials it resembles, since it is so soft that it is easily scratched by a pin or other sharp object. The stone has an oily surface and feels like soap. While the material is still used by artists for small sculpture, today's collectors search for the older Oriental carvings with asymmetrical undercut relief designs painstakingly made by hand by artists who had an excellent understanding of the material they were using and exactly how it could be worked. This type of soapstone carving appears to be a lost art today and it is fortunate that there are collectors who realize that what remains is well worth preserving.

SPORTS COLLECTIBLES

Collecting in a single area of sports can be just for fun and may cost little, or you can gather objects to match museum pieces. Often, the "just for fun" collections become important as time passes and categories become scarcer and more meaningful. Sports collections are usually specialized by a single sport and further by one type of object within that sport category. For instance, there are baseball card collectors who want all hard-to-find pictures of players. The cards were included in bubble gum packages and a few years ago were traded by children. Now, serious adults trade and buy and sell for hard cash the scarce cards that finish certain series.

Baseball collecting is now a serious hobby and has become big business, with the rarities selling for hundreds of dollars. Conventions of sports enthusiasts who collect all memorabilia are places where a lot of money changes hands. The hobby of collecting baseball cards, autographed balls, and other souvenirs of famous athletes isn't kid stuff anymore.

The earliest baseball cards were packed with cigarettes at a time when anti-smoking campaigns threatened to make smoking unpopular. There is a 1910 Honus Wagner card that is a rarity because the player did not want to endorse smoking and threatened to sue if his portrait were not removed from the cigarette packs. There are fewer than a hundred of these cards known, and many collectors would like to own one.

Although the majority of baseball cards were packed with gum by Topps Chewing Gum Co., others were given away in candy packages, cereal boxes, dog food cartons,

Among the oldest of collectible sports figures are these Staffordshire pugilists.

and other products. Today, those who saved cards from their childhood can realize financial rewards from having done so. There is now a secondary market carried on by collectors and dealers who have turned what was once a child's pastime into a profitable business.

Golf, football, boxing, hockey, and other sports also have their enthusiasts in the collecting world. Old sports equipment, awards, and trophies are collected. Pictures, autographs, and publicity having to do with the masters of each sport are also saved. Figurines of the famous players and works of art having to do with sports are wanted. Perhaps the most desirable of these items are paintings and prints of famous racehorses. The same horses that were painted by artists who specialized in this type of work in the last century were also memorialized by weather vane makers. In addition, there were songs published in honor of great

The game of ice hockey is shown on this blue-and-white Staffordshire plate.

racing horses; collectors look for those with interesting engraved covers.

Sports collectors might want Staffordshire figures of old-time pugilists or a pair of trunks once worn by Joe Louis. Big League uniforms, no matter how worn or in what condition, have recently become "hot" items. All sports memorabilia are wanted by dealers who know they can find customers for anything connected with games and events of the past. A new category of sports collecting is Olympic souvenirs. All of this new interest in sports souvenirs and collectibles appears to have stemmed from the

Sheet music cover extolling the sport of baseball, published in 1877.

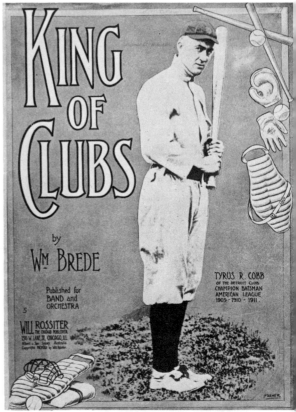

Song written to honor Ty Cobb, published in 1912, is a collector's item today.

baseball card collectors, and there is no evidence that this enthusiasm will wane.

CLUBS:

The Midwest Sports Collectors Association
15261 Northfield Street
Oak Park, Michigan 48237

BOOKS:

The American Sporting Collector's Handbook, Allan J. Liu. Winchester Press, 205 East 42nd Street, New York, New York 10017.

Baseball Cards, Gar Miller. Order from author, 400 West Cherry Street, Wenonah, New Jersey 08090.

Classic Baseball Cards, Larry Mattlin. Order from author, 70 East Walton Place, Dept. A, Chicago, Illinois 60611.

The Sports Collector's Bible, Bert Randolph Sugar. Wallace-Homestead Book Company, 1912 Grand Avenue, Des Moines, Iowa 50305.

Sports Memorabilia: A Guide to America's Fastest Growing Hobby, John A. Douglas. Wallace-Homestead Book Company, 1912 Grand Avenue, Des Moines, Iowa 50305.

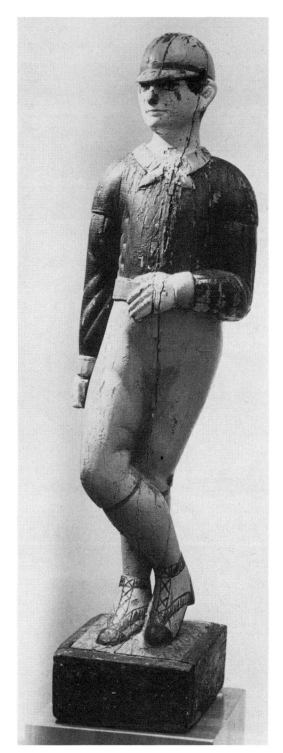

This life-size carved wooden figure of a baseball player would be a prime sports collectible.

Celluloid football doll, originally attached to a stick, was sold at games in the 1940s.

Group of baseball cards of collectible quality and era.

STEAMSHIP COLLECTIBLES

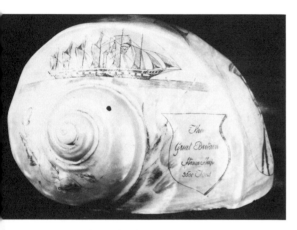

Scrimshawed shell is souvenir of British steamship.

Glass novelties from the Spanish-American War exhorted Americans to "Remember the Maine."

The luxurious floating hotels that once made ocean crossings as exciting as the Grand Tour itself have been phased out or converted to single-class cruise ships. The jet plane has replaced gracious staterooms and ten-course meals served to travelers in formal dress, and the only way to find out what luxury travel used to be like is to watch old movies or read old novels. Another is to collect artifacts from the kind of famous ships that few countries or shipping lines can any longer afford to keep running.

Transoceanic collectibles preserve the romance of luxury liner travel. Artifacts from the *Queen Mary* and her sister ship, the *Queen Elizabeth,* have been collected since the latter ship was destroyed by fire while being outfitted as a floating college in Hong Kong in 1971. The *Queen Mary* is now a maritime museum in California. Picture postcards, menus, dishes, silverware, and the Art Deco furniture that was auctioned from these ships as well as the many souvenirs sold in their shops have appeal to the collector of ship memorabilia.

While some of us tend to think of steamships as a relatively recent area of collecting, their history goes back as far as Robert Fulton's *Clermont,* the first commercially successful steamship, launched in 1807. Transatlantic steamships date from 1838. Although steamships are not as romantic visually as ships in full sail, there are models and other artifacts of both transoceanic and river steamships, and relics from both are prime collectibles. Trade cards and posters, name boards and paddle wheel covers, ceramics and glassware are all in great demand.

With collectors' ever-present interest in disasters, anything having to do with the ill-fated *Titanic* is, of course, desirable. It has

Sheet music cover records the disaster of "The Lost Steamer."

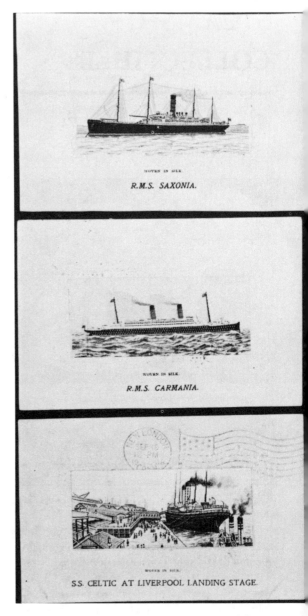

Woven silk postcards are portraits of British steamships.

been said that the Cunard Line, after the disaster of the *Titanic,* destroyed all surplus material in their warehouses having to do with the ship to discourage "morbid collectors." However, there is a story, which may be legend, that a visitor to the ship before it left the dock took a single plate as a souvenir. This plate was discovered years later with the valuable ship insignia almost indistinguishable. She had used the plate for a dog dish! We can only assume that the plate, of great value to collectors, is now among other *Titanic* artifacts.

Now that most of the luxury liners of the first half of this century no longer exist or have been converted for more mundane duty, their history is being preserved with as much zeal as the collectibles of railroading. Both represent a more leisurely way of travel when "getting there" was, indeed, "half the fun."

BOOKS:

Marine Antiques, Marian Klamkin. Order from the author, Colonial Road, Watertown, Connecticut 06795.

Photographic postcards of the great ocean liner, R.M.S. Queen Mary.

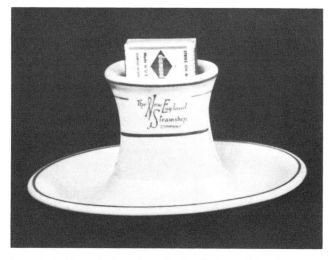

Match holder of the New England Steamship Company.
Buffalo Pottery.

STEVENGRAPHS
AND OTHER
SILK PICTURES

Stevengraph woven silk bookmark.

The late nineteenth century was a period of production of inexpensive machine-made items that fall into the category of popular art. The jacquard loom, a French invention used to weave colorful ribbons, labels, and dress trimmings, was adapted in England for the purpose of making woven silk pictures and bookmarks. These pictures, first introduced in 1879 at the York Exhibition in England, received much publicity. Visitors to the exhibition purchased enough of the first efforts of Mr. Thomas Stevens of Coventry and London to launch him in a business that produced silk pictures of hundreds of subjects. These were mounted as postcards, valentines, tops of boxes, book covers, bookmarks, political badges, framed portraits, and other items.

The intricate "pure silk woven pictures" cover a wide range of subjects, including sports, architecture, well-known personalities of the past as well as contemporary figures, genre scenes, and transportation scenes. The period of production for Stevengraphs continued to the beginning of this century. Such a huge variety and number of silk pictures eventually were made and sold all over the world that they have become an established area for collecting. While some of the rare pictures in good condition can be purchased for what seems like a huge investment when one considers the original cost, the more common bookmarks and those pictures made in some abundance are less expensive.

There were a great many Stevengraphs sold in the United States after the Centennial Exhibition in Philadelphia, where the loom was demonstrated. Americans such as "Buffalo Bill," "Mrs. Cleveland (Queen of 60 Millions of Free People)," and "George Washington" were popular subjects. These are all scarce and expensive now. The loom used by Stevens was so intricate that an entire song (words and

World War I souvenir postcards, embroidered in France, are related to Stevengraphs and collected with them.

Woven silk postcards, made by Stevens or Grant, another manufacturer working at the same time.

music) could be woven on a small bookmark and the pictures of castles, towns, bridges, and other scenes made for framing have remarkable detail.

Because Stevengraphs were widely distributed and had great popular appeal there is always a possibility that one will turn up in an old trunk or that one of the intricately woven bookmarks will be found stuck in an old book.

BOOKS:

Stevengraphs and Other Victorian Silk Pictures, Geoffrey A. Godden. Barrie & Jenkins, 2 Clement's Inn, London WC2A 2EP, England.

More examples of World War I French postcards, similar to Stevengraphs.

TEMPERANCE MEMORABILIA

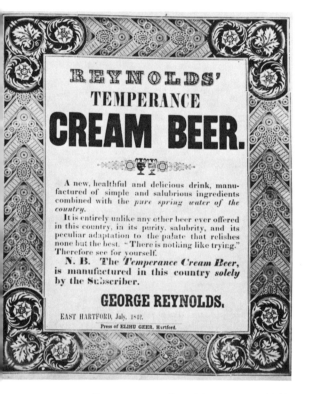

Temperance advertising poster, 1842.

Most collectors of memorabilia that represent the era between January 1920 and December 1933 when the Volstead Act was in effect are not teetotalers. They are, instead, historians of a period of American social and political history who are fascinated with the unique period of time in the United States that was called Prohibition. The collectibles include any item having to do with the national movement to curtail the sale of alcoholic beverages; these date from the establishment of anti-saloon organizations in the late nineteenth century.

Any printed material—such as programs, broadsides, or posters announcing speeches against demon rum—is wanted by temperance collectors. Picture postcards and sheet music also become part of these collections. All objects that record the life of the leader of the movement, Carry A. Nation, are especially interesting to people who are fascinated with the saloon-busting zealot who became a figure of national prominence and led an army of women who, in their righteousness, felt obligated to march through saloons and destroy everything in sight. A Prohibition Party was organized in 1869 and is still in existence; collectors want all printed material concerning its history.

There is a wealth of Prohibition items, from campaign and election material representing both views on the subject, to beer mugs that celebrate repeal of the Volstead Act with the legend, "Happy Days Are Here Again." Shot glasses with the same song title are to be found, also. There are many Al Smith and Franklin D. Roosevelt political items that express both candidates' sentiments concerning a law that was impossible to enforce.

Whiskey bottles from the Prohibition era are now collected. Most of the fancy pocket flasks, made for men and women, that are sought today are easily identified as having been made during the 1920s. Some of these are extremely handsome. They were a very popular gift item in the 1920s.

In short, all temperance and Prohibition material is in demand today. While these items fall into the general category of political collectibles, there are a great many specialists who find humor and fascination in the decade when the American government attempted to legislate morality.

Song title on shot glass is a "repeal" item that celebrated Franklin Roosevelt's election and the end of Prohibition.

Prohibition plaque asks for repeal of the Eighteenth Amendment.

Porcelain candy dish with figure of Carry A. Nation.

Currier and Ives print of 1883 which ridiculed the temperance movement.

THEATER
MEMORABILIA
AND PLAYBILLS

Theater buffs tend to save their programs. They realize that they are much more than souvenirs of performances attended; they represent the most authentic history of the theater that we have. From them we can follow stage careers of actors and actresses from bit parts to stardom. We can learn of plays and musicals that passed into oblivion and some that have become American classics. Because of their historical importance, Playbills have been collected for many years in libraries that specialize in the history of the American theater. More recently, collectors have begun to search out these pamphlets and form their own collections. Accordingly, prices for old and important Playbills are going up.

Perhaps the most wanted of all theater collectibles are original cast albums of the American musical theater. These are somewhat more difficult to acquire. Shows that had long runs, such as "Oklahoma" or "South Pacific" are not difficult to find on the secondary market, but shows of historical importance that had short runs are. Another difficulty is finding albums where the cover and the recording are in good condition. The more popular the show, the more the record was played.

Other theater memorabilia wanted by collectors today are sheet music from musicals, theater posters, advertisements and reviews, objects from sets, props, and costumes. Autographed photographs of stars and original typescripts of plays are important collect-

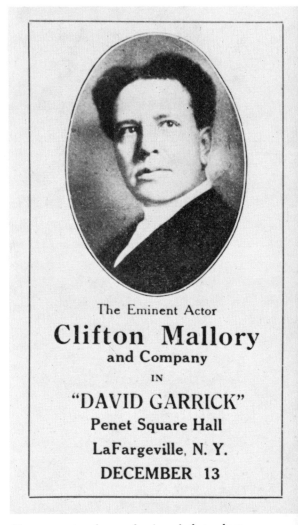

The Eminent Actor

Clifton Mallory
and Company

IN

"DAVID GARRICK"

Penet Square Hall

LaFargeville, N. Y.

DECEMBER 13

Picture postcards can be found that advertise actors and plays from the last century and the early decades of this one.

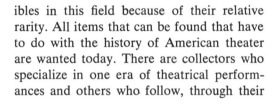

Playbills of New York musical productions of the 1920s.

Playbills of memorable stage productions on Broadway.

ibles in this field because of their relative rarity. All items that can be found that have to do with the history of American theater are wanted today. There are collectors who specialize in one era of theatrical performances and others who follow, through their collections, the careers of certain performers such as the Lunts or the Barrymores. Most theater collectors, however, look for any memorabilia that represent all of the history of the American musical or legitimate theater.

TOBACCO COLLECTIBLES

There are a lot of specialties within this broad field of collecting. They range from tobacco tins to hand-carved pipes, from objects that had no original intrinsic value to things that were very expensive when new. Cigar bands and cigar boxes are collected by many, while others buy only valuable old snuffboxes or Art Deco cigarette cases.

Within the category of cigarette cases are fabulous Fabergé cases of jeweled or enameled silver or silver-gilt, or cases made of less expensive materials such as tortoise shell, mother-of-pearl, and metals of all kinds. Decoration and design are typical of the 1920s, when cigarette smoking became fashionable for women. Artistically made cigarette holders are also collectible items from this era.

All unusual pipes are collected; some of the varieties are carved Meerschaums, American Indian effigy pipes, and Chinese opium pipes. Of special interest to collectors are pipes carved by Civil War prisoners, but all figural pipes, especially those with intricate carving, are desirable.

Snuff bottles, many made of precious or semiprecious stone such as amber, azurite, jade, or lapis lazuli, have been popular and expensive collector's items for years. They are desirable for their intrinsic value and beauty and have the added advantage of needing little space for display. These are the prime collectibles within the broad category of tobacco items; they represent a wide variety of color, materials, and craftsmanship.

Eighteenth- and early nineteenth-century snuffboxes, especially those made in France or England, are tiny works of art

Chinese snuff bottles are tobacco collectibles for those who can afford them. Many, like this one, are carved gemstones.

that have great appeal. These, too, show the craftsman's ability to adapt a wide variety of materials and designs to small box shapes. Silver, wood, enamel, and lacquered papier mâché provide the background for

Old matchboxes were decorative and have nostalgic appeal today.

all of the decorative techniques known to the craft artists of the time. Commemorative or presentation boxes are in strong demand.

Early tobacco advertising has appeal for many collectors, who search for signs, magazine advertisements, store displays, labels, and old tins from plug tobacco, snuff, and cigarettes. Tobacco premiums, giveaways, and advertising trade cards are all part of this collecting field. Most represent brands that have long since disappeared from the advertising scene, but together all of these bits of memorabilia add up to the history of a huge and influential American business.

CLUBS:

Tin Container Collectors Association
P. O. Box 4555
Denver, Colorado 80204

BOOKS:

English Snuff-Boxes, G. Bernard Hughes. Granada Publishing Company, 1221 Avenue of the Americas, New York, New York 10020.

Old Chinese Snuff Bottles, Henry D. Hitt. Charles E. Tuttle Company, Rutland, Vermont 05701.

Old American glass bottle contained Dr. Marshall's Aromatic Snuff.

Cigar store Indian, trade sign for tobacconists, would be a prime collectible. These are scarce and expensive today.

Well worn and obviously much used, this papier mâché snuffbox is a collectible object.

Political campaign pipes, made of clay, were once inexpensive giveaways, but are now important collector's items.

Pipe hand-carved by a Civil War soldier.

Tin tobacco boxes and cigarette and cigar boxes used in the past are tobacco collectibles.

TOOLS

Ice saw, used to cut ice from ponds in winter.

Old tools—those used by eighteenth- and nineteenth-century craftspeople—are a relatively recent collectible. A collector may specialize in one of many categories, or a collection may be quite diverse. Of special interest to many collectors are old farming implements, miniature tools, carpenters' tools, blacksmiths' and ironworkers' tools, and tools of the wheelwright, cooper, or joiner. The implements used in the work of the shoemaker, leatherworker, and butcher are also in demand.

In this age of mass production and plastic the implements of a simpler time have great historical and aesthetic appeal. In the old days, many workers made their own tools and prized them highly since, without them, their vocation could not be practiced. Some of the most handsome work of the black-

Handmade grain shovel was carved from a single piece of wood.

Combination broad ax and hatchet.

This "traveler" was used to measure the circumference of wheels.

smith can be found in the tools he made for himself and others. Included in this rather broad category of collecting is the blacksmith's anvil, an especially pleasing sculptural shape that is more and more difficult to find.

Collectors, no matter what their specialty within this broad category, look for tools that are handmade, that show signs of a lot of use, and that fit into their special area of interest. Kitchen and farm tools designed to do specific tasks such as pit cherries, peel or press apples, toast bread over an open hearth, or facilitate the making of candles are especially desired and, in recent years, have become more and more expensive. Tools such as calipers, log dogs, and augers are also appealing shapes that help us to understand the processes used in building houses and barns.

Some of the more esoteric collections in the category of old tools focus on tools made and used by communal groups such as the Shakers or the Amish. The Shakers, especially, put as much care into the making of their tools as they did into the products made by them. While many Shaker tools are now in museums, others come up for sale from time to time.

Related items in tool collecting are pat-

terns such as those used by the tinsmith or ironworker, trade signs, and occupational mugs. A tool collection may be small and very specialized, or one may purchase huge collections of tools that have not been used for a century or more. Recently, one collector discovered armorers' tools that had been in storage in a small town in France and bought all there were. Another collector cannot resist any handmade plane he can find. The search for the implements used by craftsmen of another era can be a rewarding and satisfying hobby.

BOOKS:

American Woodworking Tools, Paul B. Kebabian and Dudley Witney. New York Graphic Society, 34 Beacon Street, Boston, Massachusetts 02106.

Ancient Carpenters' Tools, Henry C. Mercer. Horizon Press, 156 Fifth Avenue, New York, New York 10010.

Tool Collectors Handbook, Alexander Farnham. Order from the author, Box 365 R.D. 2, Stockton, New Jersey 08559.

The Tools That Built America, Alex W. Bealer. Barre Publishers, Barre, Massachusetts 01005.

TOYS
AND GAMES

Old blocks with color lithographed nursery pictures.

The playthings of yesteryear don't have to be very old to be prime collectibles today. Just about anything made for children to play with that is no longer being made in the same materials is desirable and, in some cases, valuable. Tin windups, board games that were brightly lithographed, old teddy bears and Raggedy Ann dolls, tin and lead soldiers, early electric trains, and the thousands of other things that delighted children in the past delight the adult collector today.

If you saved that bag of marbles contain-

ing your favorite shooter and all those sparkling glass puries, somebody out there wants them. The same somebody also wants the sulphides, those marbles made with figural centers, those with mica spots, polka dots, or stripes or plaids. They want your tiniest as well as your largest marble, whether made of clay or glass. If you have any tiger eyes, they'll gladly take those, too.

Somebody else will buy your old stuffed Stieff rooster and will pay a lot more than it cost originally, but if you have a homemade rag doll that might be considered "folk art," it is worth even more than a manufactured stuffed animal, no matter how many nights it was slept with.

Old wooden blocks, Noah's arks, or Jacks-in-the-box are highly desired by grown-up, serious toy collectors who find more than nostalgia in these items. They also find a fast-growing increase in value in old-but-hardly-antique playthings. They're fun to find, to display, and to play with.

Someone out there is looking for old wooden jigsaw puzzles, paper dolls, doll dishes, and children's cooking utensils—and if you held on to that wooden rocking horse you got for your third birthday, you have a treasure desired by someone. Old dollhouses, whether made by hand or by Schoenhut, are high on the list of collectibles, as is any transportation toy or circus miniature.

There are, of course, purists in this collectible area, who purchase for their collections only toys made and used before 1900. Collections such as these include only porcelain tea sets and doll dishes that were made as early as the eighteenth century, ABC plates or plates printed with instructive maxims by Ben Franklin, and painted handmade pull toys. However, as this prime material becomes more and more expensive and difficult to find, collectors new to the field of children's toys settle for anything that has lasted since 1950.

Your Orphan Annie Ovaltine mug, your old Dick Tracy two-way wrist radio, and your Tom Mix ring, as well as any other radio giveaway, is a desirable collectible. If you held on to your Charlie McCarthy doll, he's somebody's treasure. Not only doll and toy collectors want him, but early radio buffs do, too. If you think Charlie is too new to be "old," you have no idea of what is considered desirable in this field of collectible toys. Even young adults who took care of their toys and kept them find that some of these are now high on the lists of wanted items. Howdy Doody puppets or Clarabelle the Clown items are nostalgic collectibles for an entire generation of children who grew up in front of the television set. Some people would give anything for a pristine, unused "Winky Dink and You" kit!

In many cases it is the most ephemeral of toys, those owned by kids who put things back in the proper boxes, that are high on the wanted list of today's toy collector. "In the original box" is a phrase found in toy auction lists that makes all collectors bid higher. The toy, puzzle, or doll dishes might be slightly used or worn, but all pieces must be there and the box adds value (and information). Windup toys with their original keys sell for premium prices and old Tonka trucks and Dinkey cars belong in somebody's collection. Animal toys, especially one of those popular collecting categories such as dogs, cats, owls, elephants, and frogs, frequently go to specialist collectors, but there are other customers for any zoological plaything.

All old kid's stuff is wanted by somebody today. In fact, the field of toy collecting has grown so rapidly that certain new toys are often purchased by speculators who foresee them becoming popular as collector's items only a few years after they come on the market. Some manufacturers are also astute in their ability to see the growing number of collectors among the younger generation, and juvenile collectibles are being produced in the hope that they will appeal to young collectors and their parents. Dolls are being made in series and are purchased by or for several generations.

Collectors of old toys relive childhood fantasies through their collections. Many are generous in sharing what they have collected by making frequent loans to museums and libraries where the toys of yesteryear can be seen but not touched. Others have set up their own museums, which they open to the public during the holiday season. There is great appeal and humor in childhood playthings. Some old toys display fine workmanship in products that were meant to last. Old toys made by hand were tokens of parental affection that today fall into the category of the finest kind of folk art.

BOOKS:

The Art of the Tin Toy, David Pressland. Crown Publishers, Inc., One Park Avenue, New York, New York 10016.

Cast Iron and Tin Toys of Yesterday, with Price Guide, David Pressland. Crown Publishers, Inc., One Park Avenue, New York, New York 10016.

Top, iron ice wagon is a nineteenth-century collector's item.
Middle, nineteenth-century iron fire wagon, a child's toy.
Left, tin windup, made in the 1950s, is a collectible from the television era.

Puzzle game for children.

Political windup toy has symbols of both parties beating drums.

Milton Bradley Company children's game.

A toy washing machine that really works was made in the 1930s.

"Made in Occupied Japan" windup toy has higher value if it is still in the original box.

TRADE CARDS

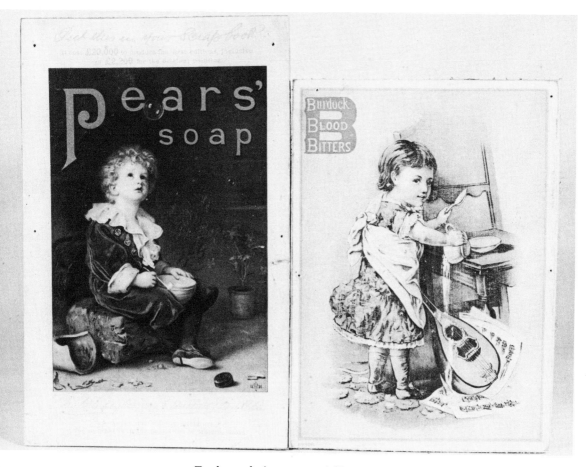

Trade cards for soap and bitters.

First came calling cards or *cartes de visite;* then came illustrated cards, first to advertise a business or service, later as a giveaway to help promote a product. The illustrated tradesman's label goes back a long way in time, but the colorful printed cards of the nineteenth century are the ones that can be found in some quantity. Most of these date from the period during the last two decades of that century when color printing and lithography were at their height.

Trade cards that were promotions for patent medicines are often snapped up by the collectors of bitters and medicine bottles as adjunctive material. Other products advertised by trade cards were packaged food, shoe blacking, household cleaners, sewing supplies, and, eventually, cigarettes. Sometimes the cards were included in the product, but other cards were postcard size and were mailed or given away at the store.

Trade cards were usually made in sets, to be admired, collected, and pasted in albums. The desire to complete their sets kept

Set of trade cards for a piano company.

A trade card advertising perfume.

the customers coming back for more and the series were often fairly large, sometimes including as many as fifty or sixty items, with all-encompassing subjects such as "Interesting Animals."

Trade cards, with a few exceptions, may still be collected without making a very large investment. Dealers can be found at large shows limited to people who buy and sell advertising art.

PERIODICALS:

Print Trader
6762 79th Street
Middle Village, New York 11379

TUNBRIDGE WARE

This Tunbridge ware card box shows the use of different colors of wood veneer made to resemble needlepoint designs.

Minute wood mosaics form intricate patterns of veneer on boxes, worktables, inkstands, card cases, and a number of other small objects made in Tunbridge Wells on the border of Kent and Sussex in England. This industry thrived from the early eighteenth century through the following century and the small gift items were sold to the thousands of people who flocked to the healing springs that turned this area of England into a great tourist attraction.

George Wise, a wood turner, started the art form in 1720 and used local woods of varying shades for his veneers. When the craft reached its peak in the mid-Victorian era, more than one hundred and fifty types of wood were used by local craftsmen. The timbers were cut into tiny strips, glued together to form a great variety of patterns, and sliced thin to use as needlepoint-like veneers. Some of the Tunbridge objects have hundreds of thousands of pieces, with perfectly matched borders and larger center

designs of stately homes and other buildings in the area of Sussex and Kent.

Popularity for spas as vacation spots waned after the first quarter of this century and, while some Tunbridge ware was made in this century, collectors look for the elaborate designs and intricately made Tunbridge pieces of the Victorian era. They look for pieces such as sewing or writing boxes that have scenes on the covers and border patterns made from a wide variety of woods. Condition is important, too, since the veneer often suffered from too much exposure to sunlight or central heating.

This Tunbridge lap desk opens from a box shape and has a secret compartment in the bottom front. Note the precise design of its veneer border.

While Tunbridge ware was not exported to any large extent, it was purchased and brought to other countries by tourists and, because of the interest of collectors, is frequently imported by American antique dealers. Tourists can find examples of Tunbridge ware in flea markets and antique shops in England, where items ranging from rulers to turned teapots are available from time to time. The making of miniature mosaics from wood is a lost craft today, and collectors who understand that the great varieties of color found in the veneers of Tunbridge ware are all natural know that the wood veneer technique is unique and will continue to appeal to more and more collectors. The paper-thin slices of wood form colorful patterns that make handsome embroidery-like pictures and borders on a great variety of objects.

VALENTINES

Valentine postcards, made before 1900, are embossed and brilliantly lithographed.

To many, old Valentines are their "favorite work of art," and are collected, framed, and displayed in quantity. These paper tokens of affection are the oldest form of greeting card and represent a holiday that has been celebrated in one form or another for centuries. The cards, themselves, evolved from single sheets of copperplate engraved messages, to lithography after 1830, to the elaborate and colorful embossed arrange-

ments put together with lace paper, bits of ribbon, or intricately folded tissue paper. It is not unusual to find embellishments of tinsel, feathers, dried flowers, or hair as part of the decoration on old Valentines.

Pre-1840s Valentines are difficult to find and are usually in museum collections, but the collector of today searches for those made later in the nineteenth century or at the beginning of this century by Louis

The sailor's Valentine is homemade of cut paper and would be a prime collectible.

This Valentine postcard is also a trade advertisement for watches and is an unusual Valentine collectible.

Prang, George C. Whitney, Elton & Co., and other giants of the greeting card business. The reason 1840 is the earliest date from which collectible Valentines can still be found is that it was the time when the Uniform Penny Postage was introduced in England. From that point on, Valentines, complete with matching elaborate envelopes, could be sent through the mail at the uniform low rate. For these early Valentines and envelopes, however, the collector must vie with collectors of postal history. United States Valentines coveted by collectors mostly fall into the period between 1900 and 1920, when German cards were at their most elaborate and American companies were making printed, embossed, and die-cut beauties to celebrate the holiday for lovers.

Valentine collectors search through old albums and trunks for just one example of a three-dimensional cardboard confection. The most elaborate of these, in good condi-

tion, can be worth up to two hundred dollars. Boutiques in fine department stores offer these at high prices during February and they are often mounted in shadow-box frames for permanent display.

During the height of the picture postcard craze, Valentine postcards were produced by the millions, some sentimentally sweet, while others were comic and cutting. These are still inexpensive and available, and are an alternative to the more expensive, elaborate cards mailed in envelopes. However, the true collector of old Valentines searches for the fancy, multilayered card that required a strong envelope to keep it together through the mail.

BOOKS:

A History of Valentines, Ruth Webb Lee. Lee Publications, Dept. J, 105 Suffolk Road, Wellesley Hills, Massachusetts 02181.

WEATHER VANES AND WIND TOYS

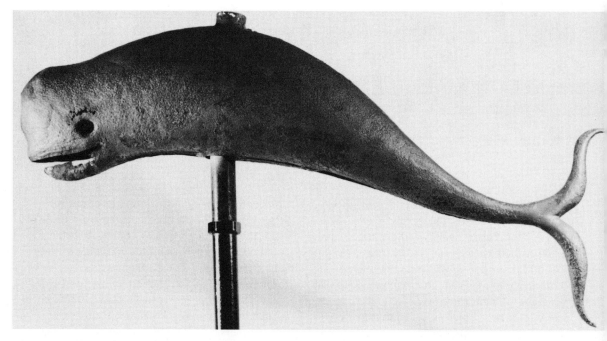

This old tin whale vane is now a museum piece and is used as indoor sculpture. Handcrafted, full-bodied vanes today are considered prime examples of American folk art.

Whether made by a home craftsman or manufactured by one of the well-known weather vane makers of the nineteenth and early twentieth centuries such as Fisk, Cushman, or Lynch, American weather vanes are now valuable collector's items. They are used primarily as indoor sculpture and wall decoration.

Full-bodied copper vanes are, perhaps, the most desirable of American weather

vanes. These were made in figural shapes of animals, train engines, automobiles, trade signs, and hundreds of other shapes. The method used to manufacture these copper-bodied vanes required a great deal of hand-work and a knowledge of the *repoussé* technique of working thin sheets of soft metal. This art form is all but lost to us today. Some of the old molds used for these vanes still exist, however, and there are new cop-

Silhouette vanes, designed by Teddy Tiffin and made by Kenneth Lynch and Sons of Connecticut, are prime examples of vanes that might still be found at reasonable prices.

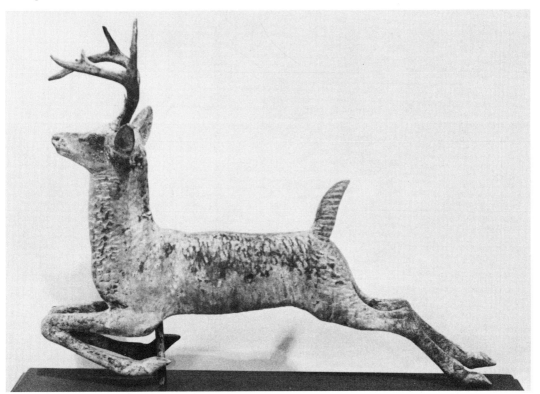

Running deer vane of full-bodied copper was made by Washburne Company around 1920.

Whirligig of a sailor with semaphore flags.

Whirligig of painted, carved wood. Paddles revolve when wind blows.

per vanes being produced today, which entices a few unscrupulous dealers to purchase them to be aged by various methods and then sold as old. However, natural aging of copper has a different appearance and a new collector would be wise to spend some time looking at available weather vanes before making any purchase.

All of the quality vanes made before the end of the first quarter of this century are worth investing in. There are reprints of catalogs of the companies that produced them so that these vanes are easily documented. Those handcrafted vanes of wood and other materials that are one of a kind are considered to be major examples of American folk art and are usually priced accordingly. When a unique handcrafted vane can be documented as having come from a particular building or as having been made by a known artisan, it will bring extremely high prices.

Wind toys, or whirligigs, are usually the products of home craftsmen. The most primitive as well as the most elaborate of these are prized by collectors of folk art. These wind-activated motion toys have been made in many styles, from the simple figure with paddle-shaped arms to a Ferris wheel with passengers destined to be forever in motion as long as the wind is blowing. American ingenuity and humor can be found in the infinite variety of wind toys seen in museums and in galleries. As folk sculpture, these are handsome additions to any primitive art collection.

BOOKS:

Weather Vanes: The History, Manufacture, and Design of an American Folk Art, Charles Klamkin. Hawthorn/Dutton, 2 Park Avenue, New York, New York 10016.

WEDGWOOD

Wedgwood collectors have thousands of objects made through more than two centuries of production. This basalt paperweight was designed by Josiah Wedgwood in the eighteenth century.

There are few casual collectors of the output of the factory established by Josiah Wedgwood in 1759. From the start, it appears that Wedgwood made ceramics geared to collectors, and that aspect of Wedgwood production continues to this day. The variety available is enormous, and there are hundreds of types of specialties within this exciting field of collecting.

Because Wedgwood creamware, basalt, jasperware, and the other clay bodies of the Wedgwood firm have always been exported from England to the United States, there are old as well as fairly recent collector's items that turn up in estate and garage sales as well as auctions. There are also several well-known specialist dealers of Wedgwood who carry rare and valuable items as well as some of the more recent issues that will appreciate in value in the future.

Types of Wedgwood desired by collectors make a long list; just a few of the specialties

can be mentioned here. Some collectors search for one or more examples of each color of jasper, while others want only the black basalt shapes. Other collectors only buy eighteenth-century creamware, that useful pottery developed by Josiah Wedgwood for dishes that everyone could afford. Other collectors only buy the bone china decorated by Daisy Makeig-Jones between 1915 and 1932 in fanciful patterns of fairies, dragons, or butterflies. Within recent years this china has increased enormously in value.

There are calendar tiles made as adver-

This basalt hare is a scarce collector's item made by Wedgwood.

This basalt boar is part of a series of animals designed for Wedgwood by John Skeaping in the 1930s.

tisements in the 1920s for Wedgwood's Boston outlet and basalt busts of historical figures. Plates made to commemorate various American historical places and occasions were made in enormous numbers and variety; this aspect of the Wedgwood business in America is still successful. One desirable group of this type of plate was designed for Wedgwood by wood-engraving artist Clare Leighton. The plates depict New England industries.

One need not be wealthy to specialize in some aspect of Wedgwood. New collector's issues include annual editions of Christmas plates, children's storybook plates and mugs, and other objects made expressly for collecting. Some of these have already increased in value more than the collector's series made by other companies less well

known for quality. The commemorative portion of Wedgwood's business has always been large and the quantity of pitchers, mugs, plates, and other shapes with printed decoration of American historical scenes or commemorating anniversaries of American heroes is so vast that one can specialize only in these. Nineteenth-century majolica is another specialty for Wedgwood collectors.

For those who like ceramics as a subject for collecting and study, Wedgwood offers variety and great beauty. It is easy to identify since almost all Wedgwood pieces are marked. Furthermore, there are usually additional marks on anything made in the nineteenth century, which makes it easy to date Wedgwood. However, because of the success of the company almost from its

Practical pottery for everyday use has always been among Wedgwood's production. Flow-blue game pie dish was made in the late nineteenth century.

Wedgwood has made thousands of collector's items for the American market. Creamware plate commemorates the completion of the Empire State Building in New York City.

founding, there are some imitations of both the wares and the mark and it is therefore recommended that the cautious collector do some reading and studying before investing in this collectible area.

If you are planning to invest a large amount of money in Wedgwood it is wise to develop a relationship with a specialist dealer who can be trusted to help you build an important and valuable collection of the type of Wedgwood that is most appealing to you. Study museum collections in order to know what the factory has made, what artists were working for Wedgwood during its long history, and what you like that you can afford.

Note: There are local Wedgwood clubs in various regions of the country and in London. The Buten Museum can tell you where they are and when they meet.

CLUBS:

International Wedgwood Society
Contact: Buten Museum of Wedgwood
Merion, Pennsylvania 19066

BOOKS:

Creamware, Donald Towner. Faber and Faber, 99 Main Street, Salem, New Hampshire 03079.

The Collector's Book of Wedgwood, Marian Klamkin. Dodd, Mead & Company, 79 Madison Avenue, New York, New York 10016.

Wedgwood: Guide to Marks and Dating, David Buten. Buten Museum of Wedgwood, Merion, Pennsylvania 19066.

WOMEN'S
COLLECTIBLES

Picture postcard making fun of suffragettes.

This sheet music, published in 1869, is an early suffrage item for collectors.

All objects that represent national social issues are, of course, the basis for many general or specialized collections. When several such issues are related to a single cause, carried on with varying degrees of success over a long part of our history, they often form the basis for small, meaningful collections and tell us more about ourselves than, sometimes, we care to know.

The struggle for women's suffrage in the United States and in England was frequently the subject of ridicule. Its outlines have been somewhat blurred in history, since the early advocates also included in their campaigns the temperance issue and Black suffrage. Nevertheless, there are objects and paper collectibles that together form an interesting history of the fight for women's rights. Sheet music, picture postcards, campaign buttons, and china are

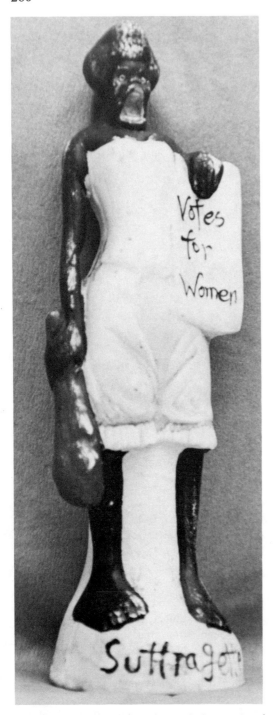

Statuette of Black woman Abolitionist and women's rights advocate Sojourner Truth.

Right, three ceramic mementos of the suffrage movement.

Suffrage movement button, a collector's item of the first decade of this century.

some of the objects that make up such a collection. One might add current Equal Rights Amendment (ERA) material to these, which shows us that the fight is not yet over.

The old sheet music dates as far back as the middle of the nineteenth century, when Amelia Bloomer lectured on women's rights. Along with the illustrated sheet music covers for "Bloomer Costume," "The New Bloomer Schottische," and "The Bloomer Waltz," a prime collectible of Mrs. Bloomer's energetic campaign for women's rights would be copies of the publication for women started by Mrs. Bloomer in 1849, called *Lily.* There were many other pieces of sheet music published, including "We'll Show You When We Come to Vote." Picture postcards of the era often show suffragettes in a derogatory fashion.

Perhaps an indication that women did not fight strongly enough for their rights are some examples of political buttons and china objects made as souvenirs of dinners. The decoration, asking for "Votes for Women" is often subdued, in good taste, and too discreet to have gotten the message across strongly enough. Other collectibles in this specialized field are programs for dinners and lectures, posters, and all campaign material dating before the Nineteenth Amendment was ratified in 1920. However, with the ERA still not ratified, this area of collecting is ongoing.

WORLD'S FAIRS

Trolley toy is a souvenir of the World's Columbian Exposition (1893).

Souvenirs of the fairs and expositions of international scope are important collectibles and often represent once-in-a-lifetime events. The first fair of this type was the Great Exhibition held in London in 1851. Most of today's collectors, however, specialize in one of the more recent American events, such as the New York World's Fair of 1939–40 or the Century of Progress held in Chicago in 1933–34. Both of these events can be remembered by the huge amount of memorabilia that is being amassed by present-day collectors who seek anything from guidebooks to furnishings of

buildings that were torn down when the festivities were over.

Perhaps the greatest amount of souvenir items came out of the World's Fair of 1939–40. Any object decorated with or in the configuration of the Trylon and Perisphere is wanted by collectors of items from the fair that had the theme, "The World of Tomorrow." As with most well-publicized events, the most ephemeral objects are often the most collectible. Pamphlets, maps, souvenir giveaways, pictures, and postcards are popular with collectors, as are the inexpensive souvenir items that were sold. Res-

"Corliss Engine Grand March" is a Centennial Exposition souvenir (1876).

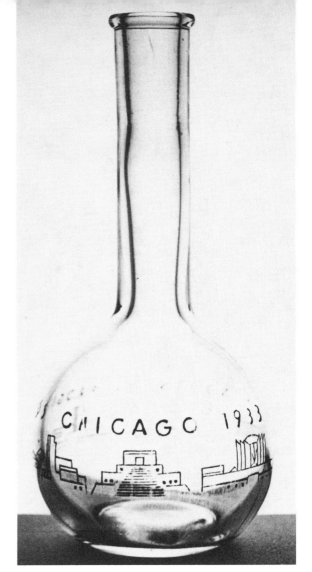

Glass flask is collector's item from Chicago World's Fair in 1933.

taurant silver, whether taken by customers as keepsakes or bought from an exhibit after the closing of the fair, is wanted, as well as any other recognizable furnishing used at the fair. Because this is a relatively new category of collecting, all items have not been listed and there are still things to be found.

There are, of course, many other fairs and expositions that have their devotees. These date as far back as the Centennial in Philadelphia in 1876. Others are the World's Columbian Exposition of Chicago, 1893; the Pan-American Exposition in Buffalo, New York, 1901; the Louisiana Purchase Exposition, St. Louis, 1904; Alaska-Yukon-Pacific, Seattle, 1909; the Texas Centennial, Dallas, 1936–37; the Golden Gate International, San Francisco, 1939–40; the Seattle World's Fair, 1962; and

there are collectors tucking away all memorabilia from the two most recent fairs in New York and Montreal. There is little doubt in the mind of anyone who has seen the current rise in value of earlier fair mementos that souvenirs of a more recent vintage will be wanted by collectors in the near future.

BOOKS:

1876 Centennial Collectibles and Price Guide, Stan Gores. Centennial Books, Box 1776, Fond du Lac, Wisconsin 54935.

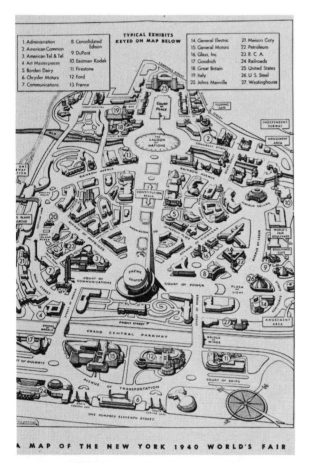

Souvenir map, New York World's Fair, 1940.

Above, guidebooks, maps, and other paper items from world's fairs are now collector's material.

Below, miniature watering can, New York World's Fair souvenir, is one of many collector's items with Trylon and Perisphere decoration.

WRITING
IMPLEMENTS

Cobalt blue master ink bottle and two smaller bottles made by Harrison's Columbian Ink.

Within the past few years there has been a revival of the art of calligraphy, and there are still a few craftspeople in the world who make quill pens. All writing implements that are pre-Bic are now collected as artifacts, and there may be some members of the younger generation who recognize pen nibs as the forerunner of the felt-tipped pen.

All old nibs and pens are worth keeping today. Collectors search for old steel nibs, first made in this country by the Shakers. Holders were made of wood, cork, steel, mother-of-pearl, silver, gold, or any mate-

rial that was practical and, sometimes, decorative. Tiffany silver pens, made around the turn of the century, are handsome, well balanced, and wanted by collectors of old Tiffany Studios desk sets. Victorian presentation pens, often found still in their gift boxes, are pretty and appealing. Some of the old pens are found today as part of a two-piece set, with the pen sitting on a pen rest of similar design.

Old pens made of glass can also be found. These were made with glass points and were so fragile that few have lasted. All of the colors and techniques used for decorative glass were used in pen-making; opalescent, clear, and multicolored glass pens have been found.

Aware collectors search for old fountain pens as well as the earlier nibs and holders. The first fountain pens, made with rubber bladders to hold the ink, were successfully made and marketed by Louis E. Waterman after 1884. Collectors search for Waterman pens and those old pens made before 1940 by Parker and Sheaffer as well. Those that were especially well made or that were handcrafted with gold or silver overlay or inlay are being purchased, cleaned, and restored as artifacts. Ladies' fountain pens and miniatures are also in strong demand.

Any writing implements that are no longer being made form collections. Elaborate desk sets were made as presentation pieces by the same companies that made the fountain pens. Many of these from the 1930s are in Art Deco style with bases of onyx or marble. The pens have large ink reservoirs and are still practical as well as

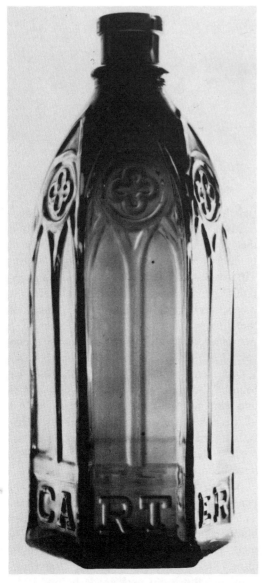

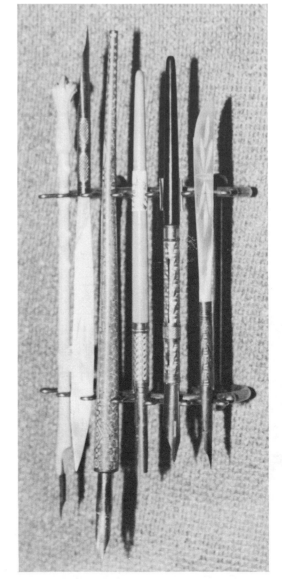

Gothic arch and quatrefoil design on Carter's Ink bottle in cobalt blue glass.

Group of collectible pens and penholders made of a variety of materials, including silver, wood, and mother-of-pearl.

handsome if the rubber bladder is in good shape. If not, an ink cartridge with a felt tip or a ball point can be substituted.

Pen collecting can be fascinating, and some old pens are still to be found in auction box lots or at flea markets. This is a collecting hobby that is still not too expensive and requires little storage space. Whether you search for eighteenth-century pen holders and nibs or the best of Water-

man's fountain pens, the variety is almost endless.

BOOKS:

Writing Implements and Accessories, Joyce Irene Whalley. Gale Research Company Press, Book Tower, Detroit, Michigan 48226.

Individual ink bottles in igloo and hexagonal shapes are early collectibles.

Ink bottles of the fountain pen era.

Advertising poster for an early fountain pen.

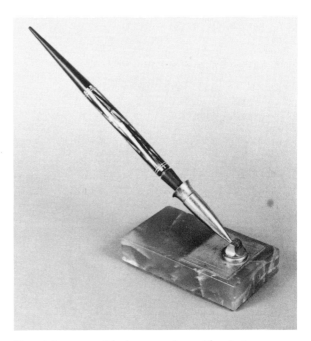

Fountain pen with brass and marble desk stand is in the Art Deco style of the 1930s.

INDEX

ABOUT THE AUTHOR

Marian Klamkin, writer, editor, teacher, is the author of seventeen books on antiques, decorating, and collectibles, is Antiques Editor for *The Lure of Litchfield Hills* and Advisory Editor to Arno Press on reprint books on antiques, collecting, and the decorative arts. She has taught courses at the University of Connecticut on collecting antiques and has acted as museum consultant on accessioning antiques.